Elegant Beading

For Sewing Machine and Serger

Sewing Information Resources
P.O. Box 330
Wasco, Illinois 60183

Sewing Information Resources is a registered trademark of Ganz Inc.

Editor: JoAnn Pugh-Gannon
Illustration: Susan P. Beck
Photography: Robert Randall Image Group

Book production provided by: Jennings and Keefe Media Development
Publishing Director: Jack Jennings
Project Manager: Janet Andrews
Electronic Page Layout: Jo Lynn Taylor
Index: Ann Leach

Printed in Hong Kong
ISBN: 1-886884-03-X

BERNINA®

Elegant Beading

For Sewing Machine and Serger

by Susan P. Beck and Pat Jennings

Illustrations by Susan P. Beck

The Bernina Sewing Library
Sewing Information Resources, Wasco, IL

Acknowledgments

Marilyn Allen for all her work to legitimize machine beading as an art form. She has devoted a great deal of energy educating the sewing world in the art of machine beading. The design used to bead the sweater dress sample is an original design by Marilyn C. Allen.

Charlou Lunsford for her help with sewing some of the samples for this book and for checking and double checking pattern directions.

Edna Gregory from Havre, Montana for the pin woven vest sample and for allowing us to share her creative use of serger trim and semi-precious stones.

Linda Brice of Mount Vernon, Washington for the use of her beaded shoulder toss as a sample of beaded elegance at its finest.

Debbie Jennings Valley for getting married and allowing Mom to design and create her wedding dress.

JoAnn Pugh-Gannon for suggesting we write this book and for her patience with us as we worked long distance to coordinate and complete this manuscript.

A special thank you to Bernina of America for the opportunity to learn, explore and experiment with all facets of machine arts and sewing techniques.

Last, but definitely not least, a heart felt thank you to our families and especially our husbands for their support, encouragement and understanding.

Introduction

While attending a national machine arts conference several years ago, Pat Jennings became fascinated with several beaded garments displayed and modeled by machine artist, Marilyn Allen. Allen's work inspired Pat to pursue this form of machine art and to attend the first of many classes on machine beading.

As Pat's skills improved and her knowledge expanded, Marilyn Allen continued to encourage and inspire her. At Allen's suggestion, Pat began teaching machine beading at seminars, machine art conferences, and at Bernina of America's dealer convention, Bernina University.

When Pat's daughter announced her engagement, it was assumed by all that "Mom" would design, sew, and of course, bead the wedding gown. Creating this gown, pictured in Chapter 9, was the greatest challenge she has faced as a machine beader.

Susan Beck became intrigued with the world of beading while attending a fashion show where she saw a lovely beaded shawl transform a classic black blazer into an elegant evening garment. As a teacher of sewing machine techniques, Susan experimented with and incorporated machine beading techniques into her many classes and seminars.

Susan and Pat soon discovered their shared interest and excitement in machine beading while working as sewing specialists for Bernina of America. This book is the result of their desire to share with you that enthusiasm.

Elegant Beading for Sewing Machine and Serger not only covers the how-tos of beading using the sewing machine and serger, but also, in Chapter 1, provides a brief history of how beads came into being and the part they have played in society through the ages. Chapter 2 offers an in-depth discussion of materials and supplies that are used in machine beading. The specifics of the various techniques using both the sewing machine and serger are outlined in Chapters 4 through 6.

After becoming familiar with the techniques, we suggest that you try them on a variety of projects. Choose any one from Fashionable Accessories (Chapter 7), Exquisite Crafts (Chapter 8) or Elegant Attire (Chapter 9). Start with the simple but elegant Black Tie Belt in Chapter 7, and graduate to the wedding gown embellished with beautiful beaded lace in Chapter 9. We challenge you to go beyond the projects described in this book, using the designs and techniques to customize and personalize your next project.

Designed to be both a workbook and a technique reference manual, this book will become a valuable resource in your own sewing reference library. As you work through the various projects, we encourage you to experiment with different techniques. We hope you are inspired to use this information as a starting point for exploring your own avenues of creativity in machine beading.

Table of Contents

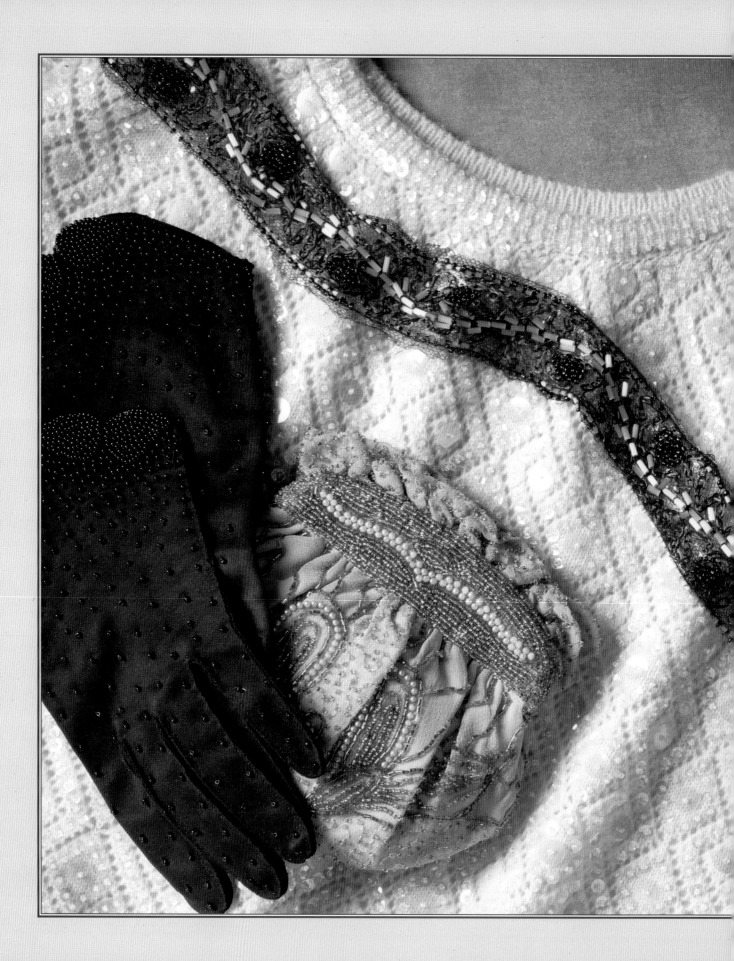

CHAPTER 1

Bead Beginnings

*A*nthropologists and archaeologists have developed intricate and interesting ways to study found objects and trace the pathways of humans throughout the ages. Common threads woven through the artifacts of different cultures are often found. An interesting commonality found in most societies is the use of beads. In almost all cultures, beads of some type were used for a variety of reasons, from the practical to the frivolous.

A Historical Perspective

Over time, the use of beads has taken on numerous faces. Not only have they been used for adornment and enhancement because of their beauty, but they also have been meaningful to humans for many practical reasons.

The word "bead" comes from the Anglo-Saxon words "bid-dan," meaning "to pray," and "bede," meaning "prayer." Rosaries or strings of counting beads are used by many of the world's well-known religions: Catholicism, Hinduism, Islam, and Buddhism. The purpose of the string of beads is to count the prayers as they are said, making sure none is omitted.

The earliest form of the calculator is the Chinese abacus, beads strung on wires for figuring mathematical computations. Some form of the abacus has been used in Japan, Turkey, Iran, and Russia, where it is still used today.

Using beads as currency is a concept most people know from history books. Many cultures used some form of beads to trade for durable goods, thus making them one of the earliest types of money. Beads took up little space and were a form of portable wealth that suited the nomadic life of some cultures.

Columbus traveled with green and yellow beads, giving them to the first people he saw after his long voyage. Unable to verbally communicate with the natives he encountered, Columbus offered the beads as a show of friendship.

Over time, beads became a symbol of prosperity and status. Citizens accumulating large quantities of beads of rare quality were the ones with the most power and authority. In ancient Egypt, men and women alike wore headpieces and collars made from strung

2

beads. Pharaohs and kings were buried with elaborate beaded aprons to help prepare them for the next life.

In some cultures, beads have been looked upon as charms to ward off evil spirits. In Asia, they are thought to bring about a good harvest, and in the Philippines, semiprecious stone beads are said to have therapeutic qualities for the wearer.

Worldwide, beads were used for personal decoration with one notable exception. In what's now known as Western Europe and England, the medieval church frowned on all forms of personal adornment. It wasn't until Queen Elizabeth I came into power in the 16th century that women, as well as men, began wearing beaded jewelry for the purpose of beauty and attraction.

Beaded clothing came into vogue during the Renaissance and has since been a staple of glamorous fashion garments. It was especially popular during the Victorian era, when excessive embellishment was the norm. Even though the beads had to be tediously stitched onto garments by hand, the style of the day showed heavily beaded bodices, skirts, bonnets, and gloves. Handmade beaded trims could be purchased, making the job of stitching the beads in place somewhat easier.

Styles of the early 1920s found the flappers wearing beaded clothing and carrying beaded accessories such as the purse shown in the opening photograph. Stitched onto a snap frame and adorned with a faceted glass ring on the front, this beaded pattern was typical of the style of this period.

American designs became a bit less flamboyant in the '30s and the '40s, but beading was still a popular decoration. The gloves shown

3

are not only hand-beaded, but also hand-stitched. The tone-on-tone beading adds a subtle textured design to these special-occasion gloves.

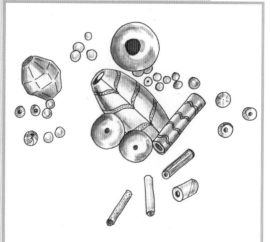

The sweater is vintage 1950s and shows the move toward beading casual clothing as well as evening wear. The relaxed fashion rules that have governed the design world since the '60s show beading on virtually any type of clothing or accessory.

Today, a bead is often thought to be a round shape with a hole through it for attaching or stringing. A bead can actually be any shape and made from a variety of materials. The distinguishing detail is the hole for attaching.

The earliest beads were made of shell, bone, horn, and other natural materials. Most societies made beads from the raw materials found locally. With the expansion of the known world and the travels of explorers such as Columbus and Marco Polo, materials were introduced and traded to other areas. As a result, beads from around the world are readily available to the modern crafter.

In earlier times, Africans used seeds, nuts, and carved bones. Today, they also make beads from hammered sheet metal and recycled

glass. They developed the process of making powder glass beads in the 16th century and still use it today. Africans also use hammered metal to make unique beads.

Chinese beads are among the oldest found—intricately carved wooden beads representing flowers and figures from their ancestry. Cloisonné beads were first developed during the Ming dynasty and are still being crafted today using many of the

4

ancient methods. Freshwater pearls made into beads come from Chinese waters.

The rain forests of South America provide expensive wooden beads made of rosewood, kingwood, and mahogany. Intricate ceramic beads are handmade by the Peruvians, jade beads come from the Mayas, and long strands of gold glass beads are worn in Ecuador.

Metal, glass, and wood are common materials used in bead making in India. Natural supplies of semiprecious stones provide a variety of beads from this culture.

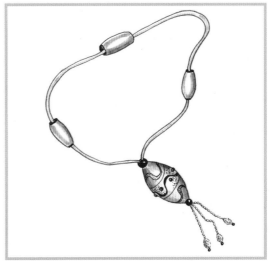

Italy is the home of the Venetian glass bead industry, which dominated the world bead trade during the Renaissance. With export trade booming around the world, copies of these beads are now found almost everywhere.

Native North Americans use natural resources, such as turquoise, coral, and silver to make beads. The Mississippi River offers true freshwater pearls to add to the collection.

Until recent times, beads were made individually and by hand, making them more precious and meaningful than today's mass-produced beads. In the latter part of the 19th century, mechanical means of producing beads made them more plentiful and attainable by almost everyone. In today's modern factories, thousands of beads are manufactured each hour from a wide variety of materials. These beads are readily available at craft and bead stores for reasonable prices. Even with such ready accessibility, designers still choose the bead as a special and elegant accent for garments, craft projects, and fashionable accessories.

CHAPTER 2

Materials and Supplies

*B*eading is one of the hand-needle arts that is easily adapted to the sewing machine. With the appropriate supplies and techniques, the movement and pattern of the hand needle can be duplicated by using an electric needle, the sewing machine.

Types of Beads

The size of a single bead is determined by measuring the distance between its two holes. Strands of beads are sized by the diameter of the bead. When gathering supplies for a project, consider the following in the selection of the beads.

Glass beads

With the variety of beads available today, it is important to understand the properties of each type. This will help ensure that each beading design is a lasting work of art.

Developed by the ancient Egyptians to adorn the Pharaoh and the royal court, glass beads are perhaps the most widely used type of bead in the world. Individually made or mass produced, glass beads can take many shapes and forms.

Small, cylinder-shaped glass beads known as "bugles" are often found in jewelry as well as on garments. Because of the small, long shape, bugles are prestrung before being stitched to cloth.

Crystal beads were first created in the late 19th century by Daniel Swarovski of Austria. Creating a machine to replace the cutting tools used in the precious stone business, he cut the glass to create a multifaceted bead known as the Austrian crystal. As the light dances off these beads, they give the illusion of a diamond at play.

Today a molding and tumbling process has been created to duplicate the Austrian crystal. The more expensive crystal is available in bead shops, and its brilliance far outshines the mass-produced glass versions.

Crosslocked beads are manufactured by stitching individual glass beads onto crosslocked cotton braid. This industrial process produces strings of beads locked together for stitching onto projects

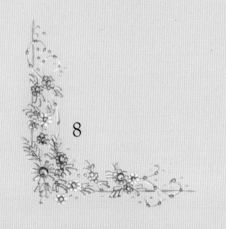

8

by hand or machine. The locking process keeps the beads from coming apart when the braid is cut. Available in a variety of colors and sizes, crosslocked beads may be purchased at craft and fabric stores.

Small round beads are known as "seed" beads. Most seed beads are glass, but the plastic seed bead is appearing more often in bead shops and fabric stores.

Glass beads come in a brilliant variety of colors. Color can be added to the bead when the glass is in the molten or liquid stage, or after the bead has been molded. If the color is within the glass, it will withstand today's modern laundering processes. Glass beads intended for jewelry or craft projects often have color finishes applied to the bead after it is molded. Test beads for colorfastness by laundering a beaded swatch of fabric before using it on a project.

Glass Pearls

Clothing or bridal pearls are glass beads dipped in paint to give the appearance of a natural pearl. The quality of the dipping determines the quality and the use of the bead. Beads intended for use on craft projects are dipped only enough to color the bead. When the project is laundered, the color may wash off the bead. If the bead is intended for use on a garment, the bead is dipped 20 to 30 times, and the paint is allowed to dry between dippings. When making beads for clothing, French and Japanese manufacturers use this multidipping process to create pearled beads that will withstand laundering and dry cleaning.

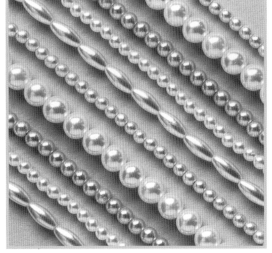

Bridal pearls come in a variety of shapes and sizes. Round and oval beads are the most common shapes. Oval bridal pearls, referred to as "oat"

9

pearls, resemble a grain of oat. Teardrops and oval disks are shapes that are also available in limited sizes and colors. Bridal pearls are packaged as individual beads or loosely prestrung on cotton thread. Oat pearls range in size from 3 mm to 10 mm, and round pearls are sized from 2 mm to 10 mm. With soft pastels or white as the color choices, the machine beader will find these beads used on elegant evening wear and bridal garments.

Synthetic beads

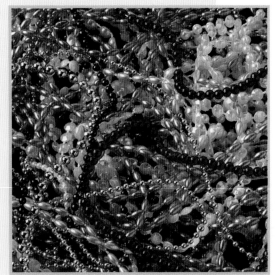

Molded plastic provides the beading artist with an endless variety of colors and shapes for beading. Many are actually plastic charms. Because it's so inexpensive, plastic has become one of the most popular bead materials available. The properties of plastic lend themselves to forming delicate translucent beads as well as metallic-looking beads and charms. Molded-on-a-string plastic beads and pearls are found in most fabric stores and are a popular choice for craft projects.

If the color is properly sealed or added to the plastic before the molding process, good plastic beads do well when laundered. Because these beads are plastic, it's best to use a low heat setting of the clothes dryer or to line-dry the item that is beaded. If pressing is needed, place the garment face down and press from the wrong side, using a press cloth and a cool setting.

Ceramic or porcelain beads

Made from clay, ceramic beads are formed into the desired shape, painted, and then fired (baked) to make them firm. A glaze to seal the clay is then applied, and the bead is fired for a second time. On high quality beads, the hole for stringing or attaching the bead is

10

drilled before the glazing process. This allows the glaze to enter the hole and seal the clay within it. High quality clay or porcelain beads are not porous and may be hand washed. Dry cleaning is generally not recommended because the chemicals used in dry cleaning may destroy the glaze finish on the bead.

Polymer clay beads and charms

Bead artists are reaching beyond what is readily available to the consumer in bead shops. Using tools found in the modern kitchen, the creative artist is fashioning beads from clay products, such as Sculpty®, Fimo®, and Curnit®. These well-known brands of polymer clay are found in most craft stores. Books and magazines are readily available at bookstores and craft shops describing the molding and baking process. Beads and charms made from polymer clay are machine washable on a delicate cycle. Items decorated with beads made from polymer clay should be line-dried to avoid heating the clay.

Sequins

Many stitchers use sequins along with beads on projects. Sequins can be made of plastic, metal, leather, or vinyl, with plastic being the most common material used. They are flat or cupped, smooth or faceted, available as strands on a braid or packaged individually, and come in many sizes and colors. Plastic sequins are either colored in the molding process, or dipped in paint after the sequin is made. The common sequin has a center hole, and the disk sequin has a hole that is off center.

11

Avoid pressing or exposing plastic sequins to heat and steam. The heat of an iron can distort the sequin shape, and steam will often dull or discolor the finish on the sequin.

Treasures

In addition to beads, items referred to as "found treasures" are often used in the embellishing process. These treasures might be metal charms, unusual buttons, or other objects that can be stitched onto fabric. Trinkets from old bracelets, necklaces, and earrings create an antique feel for the garment or project. Novelty beads of clay, wood, and plastic add a whimsical look. Mother-of-pearl buttons from grandmother's button box may give just the desired additional dimension to a Victorian gown, blouse, or glove.

Supplies

Once the beads have been chosen for a particular project, it's time to consider other supplies and materials that will be needed. As with any type of sewing project, having the right tools and the best supplies will make the job easier and the results more professional.

Needles

Each needle made for the sewing machine is designed for a specific type of fabric and/or thread. Two sizing numbers such as "80/12" appear on a package of sewing machine needles. The first number on the package, "80," is the numbering system used by European sewing machine manufacturers. The second, "12," is the system used by other machine companies. In general, the smaller-numbered needles are used for finer fabrics and smaller beads. The larger-numbered needles are used with heavier fabrics and larger beads.

12

Needles used for machine beading should be small enough to go through the hole in the bead. Have a variety of needles available to accommodate different bead sizes. Through experimentation, the machine beader will discover the correct needle size for each bead.

The type of needle needed will be determined by the fabric and the thread chosen for the project. With the exception of the smallest seed beads, most beads can be secured using a size 70/10 or a size 80/12 needle. For the smallest beads, use a size 60/8 needle.

For knit fabrics, choose a stretch needle. A size 75/11 stretch needle has a narrow shaft and will pass through most beads. If the fabric is a microfiber, such as synthetic suede, synthetic leather, or sand-washed silks, select a needle specifically manufactured for this type of fabric. Designed with a slim point, this needle allows the stitcher to sew on microfiber fabrics without damaging them.

Threads

Threads used for hand beading are generally too heavy for machine beading techniques. Thread companies manufacture a variety of finer threads, often used for lingerie construction, that are suitable for machine use. As well as being fine, the thread used for machine beading should also be strong, especially for free-motion techniques. In many cases, a single strand of thread secures the bead to the fabric.

When selecting a thread for a machine-beaded project, look for a lightweight polyester or nylon thread. Often sold in cone form, this thread is marketed for use on the serger and is suggested for constructing heirloom and lingerie garments. The semitransparent quality of this thread helps it to blend into the fabric, making it inconspicuous. A separate thread stand is recommended when using cone thread on a sewing machine.

The threads traditionally used as bobbin threads by machine artists for appliqué or machine embroidery designs are also strong lightweight threads. These threads blend well with both bead and fabric colors when used to attach beads.

For invisible stitching on laces, lace motifs, and bridal tulle, using monofilament thread in the needle and in the bobbin gives remarkable results. Choose a very fine denier (.004) monofilament for both strength and invisibility.

When used in both the needle and on the bobbin, monofilament thread gives the illusion that the beads or sequins are floating on the fabric surface. Threading both loopers and the needle of the serger with the monofilament thread will achieve the same floating appearance. Available in clear or smoky gray, monofilament thread will blend into most fabrics. Choose the clear thread when working with light-colored or white fabrics, and use the smoky gray thread to blend into darker fabrics.

Rayon and metallic threads add an extra bit of color when stitching prestrung beads by sewing machine or serger. Selecting a thread color that contrasts to the fabric and/or bead color can add further dimension to the project. For added color emphasis, stitching between each bead several times will enhance the overall design.

14

Interfacings and Stabilizers

Interfacings and stabilizers are two products with the same function—to give body and stability to the fabric. Interfacings permanently add stability, firmness, and strength to a project. Stabilizers temporarily add those qualities. In most instances, stabilizers are removed after the stitching is completed. It may be necessary to use both interfacings and stabilizers when preparing fabric for beading.

If the project directions advise interfacing the pattern pieces, choose an interfacing suitable for the application and the fabric. Beading will not change the pattern interfacing requirements. Interface the project piece before beading, especially when using a fusible interfacing. For sew-in interfacing, baste the interfacing into place, and let the beading help hold it to the fabric permanently.

Some projects in this book require stabilizers, some do not. Always try to use the lightest-weight stabilizer available to give the fabric the necessary body to support the stitching. It will be easier to remove when finished, and less conspicuous in case some stabilizer remains. Experiment with different weights, types, and brands to discover which is best suited to the project.

Many free-motion beading projects may appear to need stabilizing, especially when working on laces. Actually, the opposite may be true. Many delicate laces may be successfully beaded without the use of any stabilizer. The lace edging and motifs on the wedding dress pictured in this book were beaded without the aid of a stabilizer.

Stabilizers are placed under, over, or onto the fabric to temporarily add body. Some stabilizers need to be pinned or basted into place. Others are temporarily pressed on to the project. Liquid and

15

spray stabilizers penetrate the fibers of the fabric. When dried, these stabilizers make the fabric stiff and easier to work with.

Tear-away stabilizers

If the wrong side of the work isn't going to be seen and leaving the stabilizer on the inside of a project won't detract from its beauty or usability, use a tear-away type of stabilizer. This stabilizer has a felted paper feel, does not disintegrate while being used, and is normally removed by tearing it away from the stitching line.

Carefully removing the stabilizer will help prevent any damage to the fabric and/or stitching. Use embroidery or appliqué scissors to trim away as much stabilizer as possible. Any remaining stabilizer will become limp after laundering.

Some tear-away stabilizers can be temporarily fused to fabrics by pressing with a warm iron. This stabilizer is easily identified by the shiny coating on one side of the felted paper. The coated side is placed face down on the wrong side of the fabric and pressed according to manufacturer's directions. Using this type of stabilizer allows the machine beader to easily work with stretchy and slippery fabrics. When the work is completed, remove as much stabilizer as possible by tearing it away.

Heat-sensitive stabilizers

In situations where removing all stabilizers is desirable, the machine beader may wish to select an iron-away or heat-sensitive stabilizer. These products turn brown and powdery when pressed. It's best to test the project materials before determining if the fabrics, threads, and beads will

16

withstand the heat (cotton setting) required to disintegrate the stabilizer. If using a cooler than recommended setting on the iron, the stabilizer will take longer to disintegrate, and some of it may remain in the stitching.

Water-soluble stabilizers

One of the lightest in weight, this stabilizer is a plastic milky-colored film. The designs are drawn directly on this film before placing it on the right side of the fabric. The design is beaded through the stabilizer, following the drawn pattern. After beading is completed, the stabilizer is rinsed away, according to the manufacturer's directions. To strengthen water-soluble stabilizers, two layers may be pressed together, using a dry iron and a dry press cloth.

When working on sweater knits, spray a temporary adhesive to the wrong side of the water-soluble stabilizer to make it adhere to the fabric. This will help keep the sweater fabric from stretching as it is beaded. Trace the beading pattern onto the stabilizer before attaching it to the sweater knit to easily bead an accurate design.

Liquid stabilizers

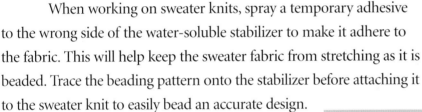

Available in various forms, liquid stabilizers are found as sprays in a can or bottle or as a paste that can be painted onto the fabric. All of them must dry completely before any stitching can begin. Use a simple household hair dryer on a cool setting to speed up the drying. After the stabilizer has dried, press the fabric. When the stitching is completed, rinse the project to remove the stabilizer.

17

Additional Notions and Supplies

18

Bead organizers

One of the biggest challenges for the machine beader is organizing the beads. Beading stores have special interlocking stacking bins to store beads. Another favorite is the embroidery-floss organizer box found in fabric and needlework stores. With either storage unit, single beads as well as strings of beads are always accessible.

When beading, use a wooden embroidery hoop to control loose beads. A piece of felt, napped wool, or velvet placed in the hoop will help keep the beads from rolling around as they are picked up. Beads can be grouped in the hoop for quick pickup. The hoop acts as both a beading palette and a container to help control the movement of the individual bead.

Beading bobbins

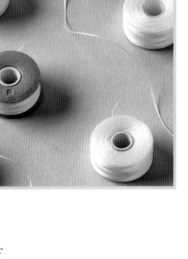

The original thread holding most beads is cotton and can be easily broken. Individual beads or beads that are loosely strung need to be restrung on a nylon beading string, which is actually a very fine cord. The most common sizes of nylon beading string are B and D, with size B most often used. Larger beads are strung on a size D beading string.

While beading string is available on thread spools, it's most commonly sold in a form resembling thread that has been wound on a bobbin. Even though it is called a beading bobbin, there is no metal or plastic bobbin upon which the thread is wound. The wound beading string sticks to itself and unwinds as the stitcher moves the beads along the string. The beading bobbin is only for stringing beads and is not intended for use in the bobbin case of the sewing machine.

Special tools

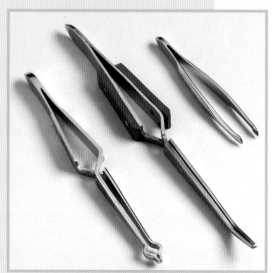

When working with individual beads, it's necessary to hold the bead in place while the sewing machine needle secures the bead to the fabric. Beading tweezers help hold the bead firmly, but will not damage the finish on the bead. Jewelers tweezers also work well. Many beading tweezers have rubber tips and a ringed groove to help grip the bead.

Beading tweezers are different from cosmetic or serger tweezers in that they open as they are squeezed. When the pressure on the tweezer handles is released, the tweezer tips close around the bead. This reverse action is much easier to control when holding a bead.

Cosmetic tweezers are useful to separate, pick up, and hold individual sequins in place for stitching. The flat edge of the cosmetic tweezer tip will permit the sequin to be held more firmly than with serger tweezers.

Needle-nose pliers are used for removing molded or cross-locked beads from their strings. It may be helpful to coat the tips of the pliers with a rubber compound found at hardware stores. The coating will help grip the bead and keep the serrated surface of the pliers from snagging the threads holding the beads.

20

Sharp embroidery and appliqué scissors are useful for clipping thread tails close to the surface of the fabric. The beveled edges on each of these scissors make it possible to cut thread tails closer to the fabric than with ordinary shears.

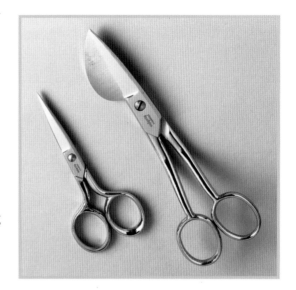

A straight-stitch sewing machine throat plate is another helpful tool that is available to the machine stitcher. The smaller, single hole offers additional support when working with fine fabrics and beading lace motifs.

Hand-sewing needles are used to bring thread ends to the wrong side of the work for tying off. A small, but useful notion is a looped-wire needle threader. It's helpful for pulling multiple threads through the eye of a needle.

CHAPTER 3

Design
Details

*A*ccurate placement of the design and motif lines on the fabric is important for any beading project. This can be accomplished in a number of ways using a variety of notions and techniques.

Choosing and Transferring Designs

The selection of fabric and design influences the choice of transferring methods and tools. Following are some of the more useful methods for transferring designs and patterns to fabric.

A light table or box is helpful when tracing a beading design for a project. Many commercial artists have large tables with a milky glass top and built-in lighting. The tables are waist high, and the artist may tip the table at an angle for easier designing. Professional light tables are often very heavy and expensive. A portable light box may be purchased at craft, fabric, and art supply stores. Small enough to fit on the top of a desk or table, this tool simplifies tracing a design. For designs larger than the surface of the box, work can be repositioned and traced in sections.

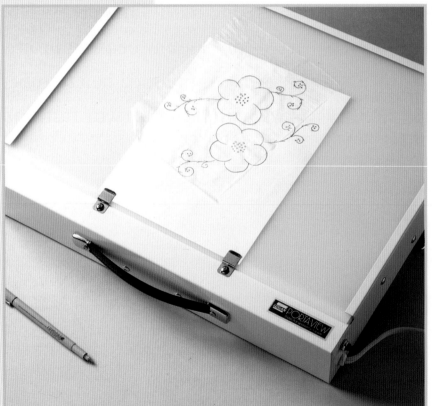

A glass-topped coffee table with a small bedroom lamp under the glass can be substituted for a light box. Be sure there is sufficient airflow around the light source to avoid heat buildup.

To transfer the beading design to fabric, select one of the many fabric-marking pens or pencils available at craft and fabric stores. Always test the marking tool on a swatch of the project

24

fabric to determine if the markings can be clearly seen and easily removed.

Water-soluble marking pens produce a colored line on the fabric. This marking line is removed by rinsing the garment with water. Sponging doesn't always remove it completely, and it may reappear after drying. Remove the line before laundering or pressing the fabric— detergent or heat from an iron can set this colored line permanently.

Air-soluble marking pens produce a light lavender or purple line. Over time this line will fade away. On some fabrics— for example, Ultrasuede®—the line disappears as the design is being drawn; on others, it never seems to fade and may need to be rinsed out. Except for the smallest of beading projects, this marker is not recommended.

Chalk pencils, powdered chalk, baby powder, or cornstarch in a pounce can all be used to transfer beading designs to dark fabrics. Take care in handling projects marked with chalk. The powder is easily erased by the movement of a hand across the fabric. If the design is large, choose a different marking tool.

Quilt-marking pencils can also be used for dark fabrics. Found in many quilt shops, these pencils come in white and a variety of light pastel colors. They are used to mark stitching designs on quilts. The marking remains on the fabric until erased or washed off. Pretest any marking pencil to see that it can be easily removed from the fabric.

25

Drawing beading designs onto a double layer of water-soluble stabilizer is an alternate method for transferring a design onto a project. Use this technique for large and/or intricate designs for easy and accurate marking. For light-colored fabrics, draw the beading design on the stabilizer with a fine-point permanent marking pen. For darker fabrics, use a white or pastel fabric paint marker. Allow the paint to dry overnight before beading.

After the design is drawn, place the water-soluble stabilizer on the right side of the project and baste or pin in place. The stabilizer may also be secured to the project by using one of the temporary spray adhesives available at craft and fabric stores. Stitch the beads to the project through this plastic stabilizer. When the beading is completed, remove as much stabilizer as possible using appliqué or embroidery scissors. Rinse away any remaining stabilizer.

Choosing Beading Projects and Designs

When choosing a garment or craft pattern for beading, first determine the overall desired effect. If the beading is to be emphasized, look for simple classic lines in a project. The beading then becomes the focal point, and the garment is only a canvas for the beaded art. If a beautifully woven fabric or lace has been chosen, use the beading to emphasize and enrich the fabric or lace's appearance.

In selecting a design for a project, there are several elements to consider. The scale and balance of the design should complement the

26

size of the project. When choosing beads and deciding motif placement, think about how the item being made will be used. Choose durable beads and fabrics for often-used articles. Fragile or delicate beads are best saved for projects that will not be handled much.

Many hand-beading design patterns found in beading shops lend themselves to machine beading. The size and type of bead being stitched may necessitate enlarging or reducing the design pattern. Be selective when choosing these designs to duplicate with sewing machine techniques. Many beads stitched by hand are tiny, and the hole is too small to accommodate the sewing machine needle. Most patterns may be used for machine beading; however, the size of the beads used will alter the finished size and change the appearance of the design.

Because few design patterns are marketed specifically for machine beading, the beading artist needs to look elsewhere for ideas. Nature, architecture, fabric prints, and lace motifs are rich with long sweeping curves and lines suitable for machine beading. Often, the design itself will suggest the bead type and placement.

When constructing a garment, decide how much of the construction can be completed before beginning the beading. When possible, try to leave the garment pieces flat to bead. It is easier to work on a flat piece of fabric than within a tube, such as a sleeve. When placing beads close to or over a seam, stitch the seam before beading.

When beading ready-made items, consider bead and design placement. Blouse or unlined jacket fronts are easy to work on, as are collar and cuff areas. Avoid beading sleeves and lined garments unless seams can be opened and linings removed before stitching.

CHAPTER 4

Beading in Any Direction

S ewing with the feed dogs lowered allows the stitcher to form intricate designs, moving across the fabric in any or all directions.

29

Freedom of Movement

Follow the free-motion instructions included in this chapter, and discover how easy it is to create almost any beaded design.

Years ago, stitchers discovered the total freedom of movement that could be achieved when they disengaged (lowered) the sewing machine's feed dogs. No longer restricted by the mechanics of the feeding system, stitchers had the ability to freely move the fabric left or right, in circles, indeed, in any direction. As a result, there was almost no restriction on bead placement. The beader simply moved the fabric under the needle and attached the bead. Techniques were developed and new areas of sewing were explored.

Free-motion machine beading requires the stitcher to remove the presser foot and allows the stitching of individual beads and charms onto the fabric. Because all free-motion beading is completed without the help of a presser foot, it's important for the stitcher to control the movement of the needle. The stitch length function is now inoperable. The distance the fabric is moved by the stitcher determines the length of the stitch. Practice moving the fabric with the feed dogs disengaged before beginning any free-motion beading project. Working with a reduced motor speed while learning to move the fabric will help keep the movements smooth and the stitching consistent. The needle-down function shouldn't be engaged for this type of work.

Strings of loose beads

Round bridal pearls, bridal oat pearls, and bugle beads are packaged individually or are prestrung on a cotton string. The beads move freely on the string and can be slid off the end for individual bead placement. They can also be transferred to a beading bobbin and stitched onto the fabric as a strand. Beads that are sold individually can be strung onto a beading bobbin using a hand needle.

30

Preparation of Prestrung Loose Beads

1. Transfer the beads to a beading bobbin. Using an overhand or weaver's knot, tie the end of the original cotton string holding the beads to the end of the beading bobbin string.

2. Slide the beads over the knot and onto the beading bobbin. (Illus. 1.)

3. Use needle-nose pliers to break off and discard any beads that will not slide over the knot.

4. When the bead transfer is complete, cut the original cotton string from the beading bobbin at the knot. Do not cut the thread holding the beads from the beading bobbin. As the work progresses, the beads will be slid along the beading string toward the beading bobbin and it will unwind.

1.

Tying-on

Before beginning the beading work on any project, it's necessary to secure the thread to the fabric. This securing process is referred to as "tying-on."

Method 1

Used when stitching molded beads or prestrung sequins, or when attaching individual beads, charms, or sequins, this method secures the needle thread and the bobbin thread to the project fabric.

1. Remove the presser foot, lower the feed dogs, and attach a straight stitch throat plate to the sewing machine.

2. Lower the presser foot lever and position the fabric under the needle. Hold the needle thread in the left hand, and take one stitch with the sewing machine. Pull the needle thread, bringing the bobbin thread to the surface of the fabric.

2.

31

3. While holding both thread tails in the left hand, move the fabric slightly, stitching three or four small stitches, and securing the threads to the fabric. After securing the threads, cut off the remaining thread tails with appliqué or embroidery scissors. (Illus. 2.)

Method 2

This method secures needle thread, bobbin thread, and beading bobbin string to the fabric. It is the method of choice when using loosely strung beads on a beading bobbin.

1. Follow steps 1 and 2 under Method 1.

2. Tie the needle thread onto the beading bobbin string using an overhand or weaver's knot. (Illus. 3.)

3. Raise the presser foot lever to release the needle tension. Pull the needle thread back through the tension disks until the knot is at the needle. Lower the presser foot lever. Lower the needle until the tip is touching the fabric.

4. Hold the needle thread, the bobbin thread, and the beading bobbin string in front of the needle. Place the beading bobbin and the string of beads behind the needle.

5. Turn the handwheel on the machine, stitching over the thread tails with a single stitch. Stitch these tails to the fabric using a bartack or very short zigzag stitch. The fabric should be moved back and forth in a rocking motion to form the zigzag stitch. Stitch over the three tails for about ¼". (Illus. 4.)

6. Straight stitch back to the beginning of the zigzag pattern and clip the loose thread tails close to the fabric surface with appliqué or embroidery scissors.

3.

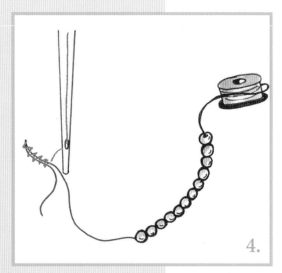

4.

32

Tying-off

After completing the beading on a project, it's necessary to knot or secure the thread to the fabric. This securing at the end of a beading technique is referred to as "tying-off."

Method 1

Used when fabric and thread color do not match well, this method is the least conspicuous on the right side of the fabric.

1. When the beading is complete, lift the presser foot lever to release upper-thread tension, and remove the project from under the needle.

2. Slide the extra beads along the beading bobbin string toward the beading bobbin and away from the project.

3. Cut the beading string, needle thread, and bobbin thread, leaving a 6" to 8" tail on each.

4. Using a hand needle, bring the beading string and the needle thread to the back of the project and secure the threads to the fabric with several small hand stitches. Thread the bobbin thread through the eye of the hand needle, and secure it to the fabric in the same manner. (Illus. 5.)

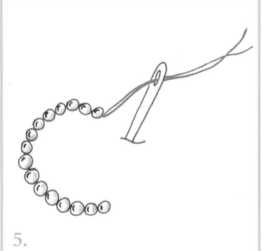

5.

Method 2

The quickest method of tying-off all three thread tails, this technique is used when the thread color matches the beads and/or the fabric. The thread may be visible on the right side of the fabric, so color matching will be important.

1. When the beading is complete, lower the needle into the fabric at the end of the last bead. Slide the extra beads along the beading string toward the beading bobbin and away from the needle.

33

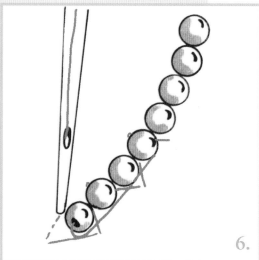

6.

2. Lay the beading bobbin string next to the beads that have been stitched to the fabric. Pull slightly on the beading bobbin string, bringing it close to the beads.

3. Stitch back over the beads, stitching over the beading bobbin string. Stitch backwards for about 1", jumping back and forth between the beads and over the beading bobbin string.

4. Stitch forward to the end of the secured beads, jumping back and forth between the beads and over the beading bobbin. Take several very small, straight stitches next to the line of beads. (Illus. 6.)

5. Lift the presser foot lever to release the upper thread tension, remove the work from under the needle, and using appliqué or embroidery scissors, clip the thread tails close to the surface of the fabric.

Method 3

This method works well for single beads, molded beads, crosslocked beads, and charms.

1. When the beading is completed, take several small stitches next to the beads to tie-off the thread.

2. Using appliqué or embroidery scissors, clip the thread tails close to the surface of the fabric.

Free-motion techniques

Attaching Single Beads 6 mm or Smaller

Single beads up to 6 mm in size can be individually attached if the hole in the bead is large enough to allow the needle to pass through the bead. Longer beads or beads that have small holes will need to be strung onto a beading bobbin before couching them to fabric (see page 31).

34

1. Remove the presser foot, lower the feed dogs, and attach a straight stitch throat plate to the sewing machine. Place the fabric to be beaded under the needle and lower the presser foot lever.

2. Tie-on to the fabric using Method 1, page 31.

3. Holding beading tweezers in the left hand, pick up and hold a bead. Place the bead one bead length from where the thread is tied-on to the fabric, and bring the needle to the bead by moving the fabric. Remember, the length of a bead is the distance between its two holes.

4. With the bead on the fabric surface and its hole facing the needle, lower the needle into the bead by turning the sewing machine's handwheel. Always bring the needle down to the bead. Do not place the bead on the needle—place the needle into the bead. Using the foot control, complete the stitch. (Illus. 7.)

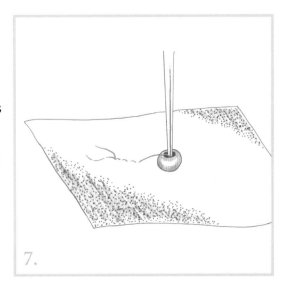

7.

5. Move the fabric so the needle is directly over the original securing point, and take a single stitch. The bead will roll onto its side and be secured to the fabric. On a quality beaded project, the hole in the bead should not be seen. (Illus. 8.)

6. Continue to attach single beads until the beading is complete. If the thread will be visible on the surface of the fabric, it is necessary to tie-off using Method 1, page 33, after attaching each bead. If the thread is easily concealed in the design of the lace, use a running straight stitch to move to the area where the next bead is to be attached.

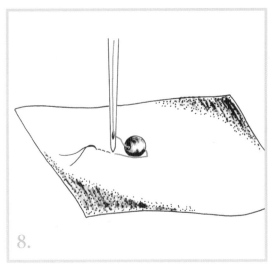

8.

7. When the design is complete, tie-off using Method 3, page 34.

Attaching Single Beads Larger Than 6 mm

Single beads larger than 6 mm in size need to be prestrung onto a beading bobbin before attaching them to the project.

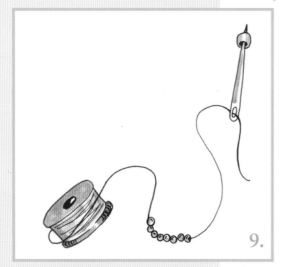

9.

1. If the beads are on the original cotton string, transfer the beads to a beading bobbin following the instructions under "Preparation of Prestrung Loose Beads," page 31. For individual beads, use a hand needle to string them onto the beading string. (Illus. 9.)

2. Using the appropriate method from Chapter 3, transfer the beading design to the fabric.

3. Remove the presser foot, lower the feed dogs, and attach a straight stitch throat plate to the sewing machine. Place the fabric to be beaded under the needle and lower the presser foot lever. Tie-on using Method 2, page 32.

4. Slide the loose beads away from the needle on the beading bobbin string.

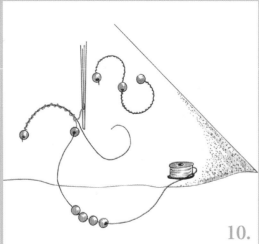

10.

5. Lay the beading bobbin string along the design, and free-motion zigzag over the string until you are at the placement for the first bead. (Illus. 10.)

6. Move a bead along the beading bobbin string up to the needle. Hold the bead and move it to the right or left of the needle's path, carrying the beading bobbin string with the bead. Straight stitch the length of the bead, leaving the needle in the fabric.

7. Lay the beading bobbin string in front of the needle, and stitch across, but not into, the beading bobbin string.

8. Pull the beading bobbin string away from the needle, sliding the bead into place. Zigzag over the beading bobbin string to the next placement point.

36

9. Repeat steps 6 through 8 until the beading is complete.

10. Tie-off using Method 1, page 33.

Attaching Charms, Single Sequins, and Treasures

Charms and other small treasures can easily be attached by the sewing machine if they have a hole or some type of opening in them.

1. Using the appropriate method from Chapter 3, transfer the design to the fabric. Remove the presser foot, lower the feed dogs, and attach a straight stitch throat plate to the sewing machine. Place the fabric under the needle and lower the presser foot lever. Tie-on to the fabric using Method 1, page 31.

2. Position and hold the charm on the fabric with a glue stick. Place the needle into the hole on the charm by turning the handwheel. Using the foot control, complete the stitch.

3. Move the fabric so that the next stitch will be off the charm and onto the fabric. After stitching into the fabric, move the hole in the charm back under the needle, and stitch into the charm's hole again. Repeat this technique until the charm is securely attached. As a decorative accent, fan the stitching. The stitch in the hole will always be in the same place, but the stitch onto the fabric is fanned around the hole's opening. (Illus. 11.)

11.

4. Continue stitching in the direction of the next charm, sequin, or treasure, and repeat steps 2 and 3. Tie-off using Method 3, page 34. (Illus. 12.)

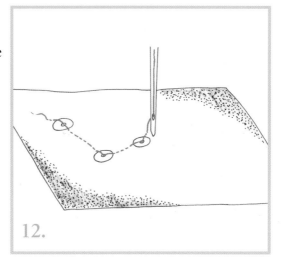

12.

Attaching a String of Loose Beads in a Straight Line

1. Using the appropriate method from Chapter 3, transfer the beading design to the fabric.

2. Remove the presser foot, lower the feed dogs, and attach a straight stitch throat plate to the sewing machine. Place the fabric under the needle, and lower the presser foot lever. Tie-on using Method 2, page 32.

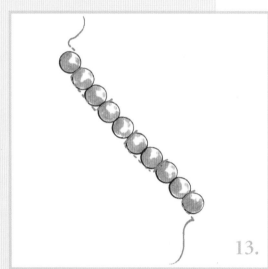

3. Lower the needle into the fabric, and bring the string of beads in front of the needle.

4. Slide most of the beads away from the needle, toward the beading bobbin. Leave 1" to 1½" of beads close to the needle.

5. Slide this short length of beads along the beading bobbin string to where the thread is attached to the fabric. With the beads lying flat on the fabric and snug against the last stitch, take several stitches on one side of the string of beads, stitching past one or two beads.

13.

6. Move the needle over the string of beads. The needle thread will need to lie between two beads. Straight stitch along the other side of the string of beads past one or two beads.

7. Move the needle back across the string of beads and continue stitching. Moving the needle back and forth across the string of beads is referred to as "jumpstitching." (Illus. 13.)

8. Repeat this exercise until the beading is completed.

9. While jumpstitching, slide the extra beads along the beading string toward the beading bobbin. The beading bobbin will unwind to accommodate the beads. Keep only a few beads snug against the last stitching. Move more beads to the needle as they are needed.

10. Tie-off using Method 1, page 33 or Method 2, page 33.

Attaching a String of Loose Beads in a Curve

1. Follow Steps 1 through 4 from "Attaching a String of Loose Beads in a Straight Line," page 38.

2. Slide the short length of beads along the beading string to where the thread is attached to the fabric. Form the beads into the curve.

3. With the beads lying flat on the fabric and snug against the last stitch, take several stitches on the inside of the curve, next to the string of beads.

4. Move the needle across the string of beads and take a stitch. Move the needle back across the string of beads without any forward motion and take a stitch.

5. Take several stitches along the inside of the curve. Jumpstitch across the string of beads and take a single stitch. Jumpstitch back across the string of beads and take a single stitch. (Illus. 14.)

6. Take several stitches along the inside of the curve.

7. Continue to stitch, always keeping any forward movement to the inside of the curve.

8. When the beading is complete, tie-off using Method 1, page 33 or Method 2, page 33.

14.

Attaching Bangles

Bangles are hanging loops of beads that add movement and character to any beaded project.

1. Thread the beads to be used for the bangles onto a beading bobbin.

2. Using the appropriate method from Chapter 3, transfer the beading design to the fabric.

39

15.

3. Remove the presser foot, lower the feed dogs, and attach a straight stitch throat plate to the sewing machine. Place the fabric under the needle and lower the presser foot lever.

4. Tie-on using Method 2, page 32, leaving the needle down in the fabric.

5. Slide the beads along the beading bobbin string and away from the needle.

6. Determine how many beads you wish to have hanging in the bangle. Slide these beads along the beading string toward the needle stopping 2"– 4" from the needle.

7. Bring the beading bobbin string at the end of the selection of beads in front of the needle forming a dangling loop. Stitch back and forth across the beading bobbin string three times. Do not stitch into the beading bobbin string. (Illus. 15.)

8. Pull on the beading bobbin string to snug the hanging beads into position.

9. Using a free-motion zigzag stitch, stitch over the beading string to the next placement position.

10. Repeat steps 6, 7, and 8 until all bangles are attached. Tie-off using Method 2, page 33.

Attaching Treasures without Holes

Occasionally an object without a hole would be perfect for a beading project. While technically not beads, these treasures can be attached to the fabric by surrounding them in thread using machine bobbin work. It is recommended that a second bobbin case for the machine be used for all bobbin case work. The bobbin case that comes with the sewing machine has the tension set for a balanced stitch using regular-weight sewing thread. If the original bobbin case is adjusted for bobbin case work, it may need to be readjusted by a sewing machine

40

mechanic to find the proper tension setting for a balanced stitch.

1. Wind a bobbin with a fine decorative rayon or metallic thread.

2. Loosen the second bobbin case tension screw. This will allow the bobbin thread to be pulled easily to the top side of the fabric. (Illus. 16.)

16.

3. Remove the presser foot, lower the feed dogs, and attach a straight stitch throat plate to the sewing machine.

4. Thread the needle with a polyester thread and tighten the upper tension. This tighter tension will pull the bobbin thread to the top side of the fabric.

5. Place the fabric under the needle, and position the object to be encased on the fabric, holding it in place with a glue stick.

6. Lower the presser foot lever. While holding the needle thread, take one stitch and pull the bobbin thread to the top side of the fabric.

7. Hold the thread tails and begin straight stitching around the object to be encased. Space the first row of stitches about ¼" apart. The bobbin thread will come up onto the top side of the fabric, and the needle thread will pull the bobbin thread up and over the object. (Illus. 17.)

17.

8. Stitch around the object again, placing the stitches closer together.

9. Tie-off all threads using Method 2, page 33.

41

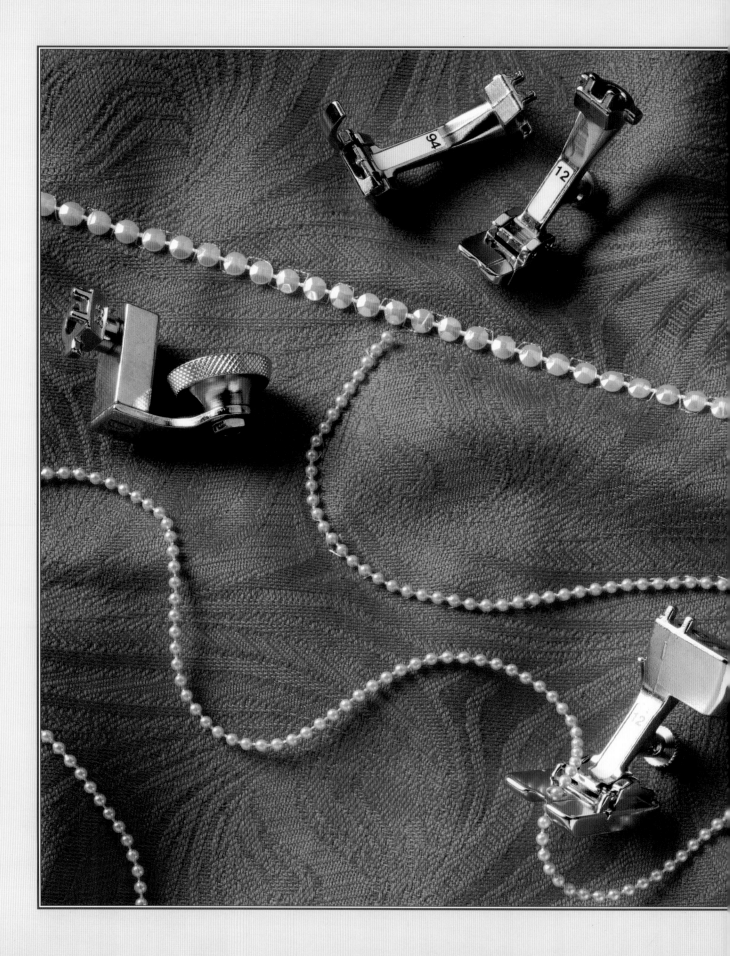

CHAPTER 5

Following a Path

Beading with a presser foot is a simple way to attach crosslocked, molded, or almost any type of strung beads or sequins to fabric. It can be an easy technique for adding decorative accents to special projects. Individual beads can only be attached with a free-motion stitching technique.

Selecting the
Proper Presser Foot

With the help of specially designed presser feet, attaching strung beads to fabric is as easy as sewing a zigzag stitch.

Sewing machines are designed to create stitches across the surface of fabric by guiding the cloth under the needle. The path the fabric follows is generally a straight line; however, it can easily be manipulated to stitch gentle curves and specific shapes. When stitching beads onto the fabric, simply choose the correct stitch and presser foot for the type of beads selected. Once the machine is properly set up, the machine does all the work.

Unlike beading without a foot, where the design can be followed in any direction, beading with a foot requires some consideration and understanding of the sewing machine and its presser feet.

Sewing machines have small movable teeth called "feed dogs" that move in a front-to-back motion. Working in conjunction with the pressure of the presser foot, the feed dogs pick up the fabric and transport it to the back. As the foot control is pressed, the feed dogs will continuously repeat this cycle, feeding fabric in a smooth, repetitive manner. Because of this straight-line movement, designs that have tight, closed loops and turns will be difficult, if not impossible, to execute easily. Those designs are best stitched using the free-motion technique described in Chapter 4.

Since the invention of the sewing machine in 1859, numerous presser feet and attachments have been developed to expand its capabilities. When stitching over objects placed on the surface of the fabric, such as a strand of beads or sequins, it is

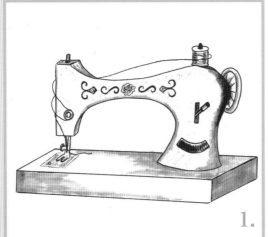

1.

44

essential to choose a foot that will allow the objects to pass under the foot smoothly and easily. There are several presser foot choices available for machine beading. The beading design as well as the type of bead or sequin being stitched to the fabric will determine the presser foot used.

Bernina Foot #12 or 12C—
Bulky Overlock Foot

Designed to be used with bulky knit fabrics, this foot has a tunnel on the sole to control the edges of heavy sweater knits. (Illus. 2.) This tunnel accommodates prestrung pearls and beads up to about 3 mm in size. The 12C foot, designed for the model 1630, has a larger tunnel and wider stitch width, and can handle beads up to 5 mm in size. If in doubt, slide the strand of beads under the foot. Move the beads back and forth. If they move without obstruction, this foot will accommodate the selected beads.

Bernina Foot #20 or 20C—
Open Embroidery Foot

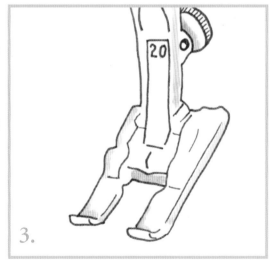

Perfect for stitching sequins in place, this foot is cut away between the toes in front for optimum visibility when following a pattern or design. The sole of this foot has a wedge-shaped indentation, allowing it to pass over full embroidery patterns and designs. (Illus. 3.) Flat sequins on a strand can easily be placed under this foot and sewn onto fabric. Choose foot #20 when couching sequins measuring up to 4 mm. For Bernina machines with a 9 mm stitch width, choose foot #20C for larger, wider sequins.

45

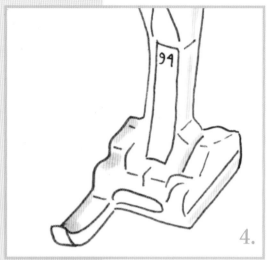

4.

Bernina Foot #94—Bias Binder Foot

Designed to be used with the bias-binder attachment, this foot has only one toe. (Illus. 4.) The unique design of this foot is perfect for attaching flat, strung sequins to the project, but it isn't used for attaching beads.

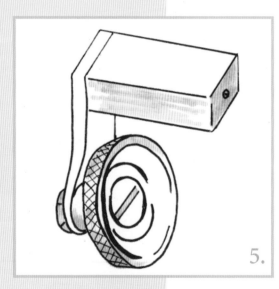

5.

Bernina Foot #55—Leather Roller Foot

The unusual appearance of this foot makes some stitchers pass it up without exploring the possibilities that it affords. Designed to roll effortlessly across leather without marring the surface, it actually gives an intermediate option in beading and quilting. (Illus. 5.) This foot works along with the feed dogs, so the machine is moving the fabric. The position and design of the roller allows the turning of the fabric in all directions, making almost any design easy to follow. It combines the ease of machine feeding with the flexibility of free-motion stitching. Because the beads pass next to, not under, this foot, almost any size of strung beads or pearls can be stitched onto the fabric.

46

Bernina Foot #30— 3-Groove Pintuck Foot

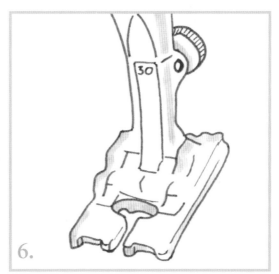

6.

This foot is intended to be used when stitching pintucks on heavy fabric. There are three grooves on the sole of this foot. Perfect for stitching rows of small pre-strung beads side by side, the previously stitched strand rides in the groove to the left or right of the needle. (Illus. 6.) The strand of beads being sewn fits in the center groove. Because the beads fit snugly in the grooves with little room for side-to-side movement, straighter lines can be beaded. The size of the bead is limited to those that will move easily through the grooves on the sole of the foot.

Stitch by Stitch

Beads or sequins are secured to fabric by stitching over them with needle and thread. Often referred to as "couching," this technique is actually borrowed from hand embroidery and is a method of stitching over decorative cords. For machine beading, beads or sequins replace the cord and are stitched to fabric using one of several sewing machine stitches. Envisioning the finished project will help the stitcher to select the appropriate stitch. The stitch may be a decorative stitch that adds to the overall look of the beads or a simpler stitch with less thread, which will allow the bead to be the focus of the design.

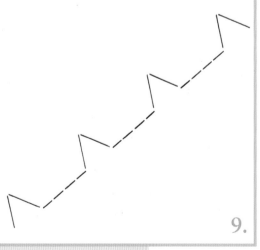

7.

The most basic stitch that can be selected is the *zigzag stitch*. (Illus. 7.) The zigzag stitch, along with monofilament thread will invisibly attach almost any bead or sequin strand to fabric. Adjust the width of the zigzag to ensure that the needle clears the beads or sequins. For beads, the stitch length should be approximately the length of one bead, so the thread will slide between the beads and be as inconspicuous as possible. For sequins, use a medium stitch length of about 2–3 mm.

The *universal stitch* is a second choice for sewing on beads and sequins. (Illus. 8.) This stitch will straight stitch along the side of the strand for three stitches, and then zigzag over the bead or sequin. After straight stitching three stitches on the opposite side, it will zigzag back across the strand. Less thread lies across the beads or sequins, making it the most inconspicuous of all the machine stitches.

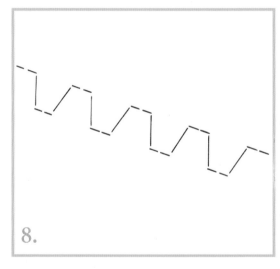

8.

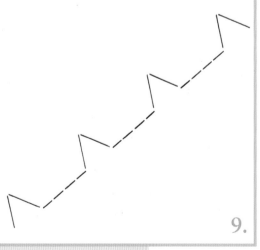

9.

The *blindstitch* will also work well to stitch a strand of beads or sequins in place, offering a floating appearance to them. (Illus. 9.) A straight stitch forms down the side of the strand, with a zigzag every 4 or 5 stitches. If the stitch is pulling tightly at the zigzag, loosen the top tension slightly to help the beads lie smoothly on the surface of the fabric.

48

The *ladder stitch* actually seems to enclose a strand of beads with thread, going down the sides and across the beads. (Illus. 10.) This stitch is a good choice if the thread is being used as an accent to the bead. Using a contrasting rayon, cotton embroidery, or metallic thread will provide a background upon which the beads will be featured. The stitch width should be slightly wider than the width of the bead, and the stitch length will work best if it is approximately the length of the bead. The cross thread will then slide between the beads, adding to the background effect. Using this stitch with a strand of sequins will give a woven effect, making it appear as if the sequins are woven into a trim or braid.

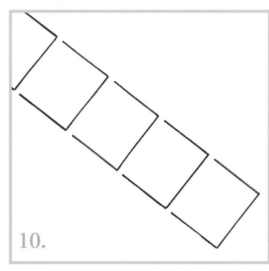

10.

Following the Design

When selecting designs for presser foot beading, keep in mind that the foot has to have room to be maneuvered along the pattern lines. Because of this, extremely close or tight designs are not good choices. Once the foot and stitch selection has been made, the techniques for couching strung beads or sequins is basically the same unless the Leather Roller Foot #55 is chosen.

Basic couching directions using foot #12, #12C, #20, #20C, or #94:

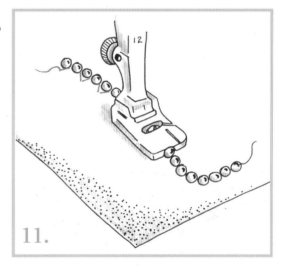

11.

1. Select the appropriate foot for the chosen bead or sequin. (Illus. 11.)

2. Set the machine for straight stitch with a stitch length of 0.5 mm. Take 3 or 4 stitches to secure the thread to the fabric, then set the machine for the chosen stitch, adjusting the length and width for the selected bead or sequin.

49

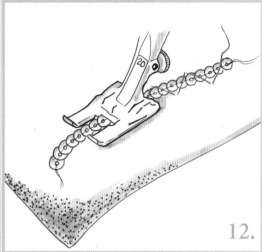

12.

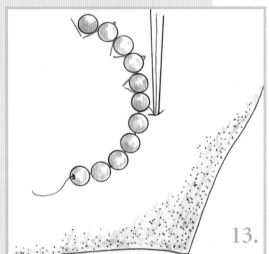

13.

3. Place the strand of beads or sequins under or through the presser foot. Sequins should be lying with the "nap" facing forward so that the foot will ride smoothly over the strand. (Illus. 12.)

4. Stitch over the beads or sequins, couching them to the fabric.

Curves

Basic sewing knowledge of stitching curves and shapes is needed when following a design using the feed dog mechanism of the machine.

When stitching gentle curves, it may be necessary to stop frequently and pivot slightly to achieve a smooth round curve. The tighter the curve, the more frequently adjustments will have to be made.

Outside curves: Stop with the needle down on the outside of the beads. Raise the foot and pivot slightly. Lower the foot and continue sewing. (Illus. 13.)

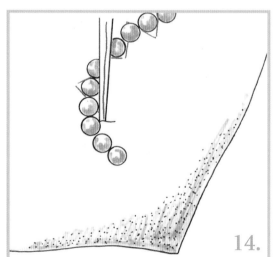

14.

Inside curves: Stop with the needle positioned on the inside of the beads to pivot. (Illus. 14.)

50

Beading Finished Edges

Edges can be embellished in much the same way as stitching beads to the surface of the fabric. The difference is that the needle swings across the bead and into the air on the other side. This technique is used on finished edges, such as a hemmed sleeve or a faced neckline. (Illus. 15.)

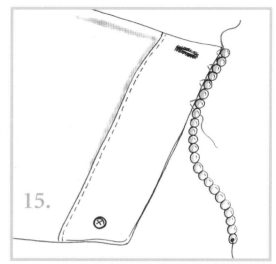

Beading with the Leather Roller Foot #55

When using this foot, the beading design can be more intricate, involved, and still be followed. The beads or sequins actually lie beside the foot rather than under it, so larger beads may also be used.

1. Set the machine for a straight stitch length of 0.5mm. Take 3 or 4 stitches to secure the thread to the fabric.

2. Set the machine for the zigzag stitch, adjusting the length and width for the selected bead or sequin.

3. Set the needle to the far left needle position.

4. Place a strand of beads or sequins to the right of the presser foot. The needle should be between the roller and the strand of beads or sequins.

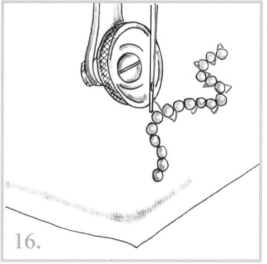

5. Stitch over the beads or sequins, turning and moving the fabric as needed to follow the design. (Illus. 16.)

51

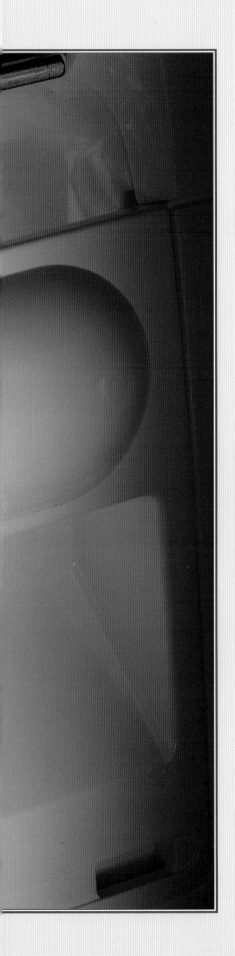

CHAPTER 6

Beading with the Serger

The overlock machine, commonly referred to as a "serger," was first used in apparel factories to produce clothing. Designed for stitching, trimming, and clean-finishing garment seams, sergers have been used commercially since the early 1900s. Sergers were first introduced into the home sewing market in the early 1970s for use by professional dressmakers and those in cottage industries. It wasn't until the mid-1980s that major sewing machine manufacturers began including sergers in their line of household machines.

Serger Tips

Home sewers have discovered how fast and easy sergers are to use. As technological developments have made sergers easier to operate, serger users have discovered additional uses for this marvelous machine. Attaching beads and sequins are tasks in which home sergers excel.

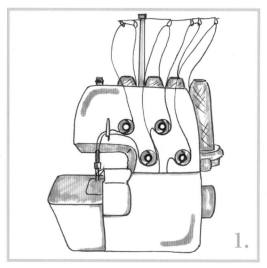

1.

Tension adjustments

Consult the owner's manual for tension adjustments for each of the stitch formations listed in the serger techniques for beading and attaching sequins.

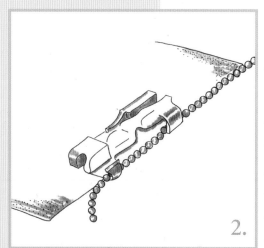

2.

The presser foot

The standard presser foot on a serger has a broad, flat sole to aid the feed dogs in moving the fabric from front to back. Because of its flat design, this foot does not allow beads and sequins to move freely under it. If the presser foot is removed to attach strands of beads or sequins, the stitcher has to move the beads or sequins to the right of the needle while trying to the keep the fabric straight and moving it under the needle at an even rate. Results are, at best, marginally successful. A consistently even stitch length is difficult to maintain when serging without a presser foot. Discouraged serger owners asked the machine manufacturers to address the challenges facing those who wished to bead by serger. To answer the need, Bernina along with others designed a special presser foot allowing beads, sequins, and cord to be successfully and easily stitched by the serger.(Illus. 2.)

54

The channel on the right side of the foot is designed to hold prestrung beads and sequins in place while serging. The beads and sequins are laid in the channel and under the small tunnel at the back of the foot. Beads up to 5 mm in size will move easily through this foot. Sequins up to 5 mm in size can be used. As the serger needle stitches to the left of the strung beads or sequins, the loopers lock the beads and sequins into the stitch.

Supplies

Needle type and size is determined by the fabric. It is wise to change the needle often. A bent, burred, or dull needle can catch on the fabric as it stitches and can damage the project.

Thread choice is based on its purpose in the project. If the beads are to be the focal point, use a fine (.004) invisible monofilament thread in needle and loopers. The beads, encased in the invisible thread, appear to float on the fabric.

If the thread is used to add color, contrast, and/or depth to the beading, consider using lightweight rayon or metallic threads for the needle and loopers. Adjustment of tensions may be necessary to accommodate these finer threads. Loosen the tensions slightly and in small increments during testing. If a heavy decorative thread is used in the looper, loosen the looper tension to create a balanced stitch.

When applying sequins, choose invisible monofilament thread or a metallic thread that matches the sequins.

Beads

Choose beads that have been molded on a string or crosslocked onto a braid for use with the serger. Their sizes range from 2 mm to 6 mm, with 4 mm being the most common size for molded beads and 2 mm for locked beads. Bead shapes are usually round or small squares. Oblong molded drops are also available.

55

Applying Prestrung Beads onto a Finished Edge

Select this technique when serging beads onto the edge of fabric. The beads will lie on the fabric, not over the edge.

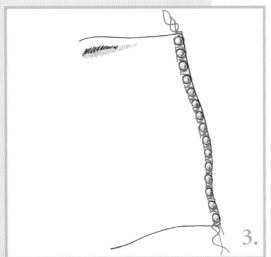

3.

1. Thread and adjust the tensions on the serger for a balanced 3-thread stitch using the right needle.

2. Raise the knife out of the way. Lay the prestrung beads in the channel at the front of the foot and through the tunnel in the back of the foot. Lower the foot and take two or three stitches over the strand of beads.

3. Raise the foot and place the fabric's finished edge, right side up, under the foot. Lower the foot.

4. Stitch length is determined by the size of the bead; a shorter length for smaller beads, longer for larger beads. If a lightweight decorative thread is being used to add color to the project, choose a short length, allowing more thread to lie between the beads. If a heavy decorative thread is being used to surround the bead with color, adjust the stitch length to encase a single bead with each stitch. Serge the beads in place. (Illus. 3.)

5. When serging is completed, bring the thread tail ends to the back of the project and secure.

Applying Prestrung Beads off the Finished Edge

Use this technique when applying prestrung beads off the edge of a project such as a collar, cuff, purse, vest openings, or bridal veil. If available, use the serger's free arm for easier application when working in a cylinder.

1. Thread the serger for a 2- or 3-thread stitch using the right needle. Adjust or change the needle plate/stitch finger. Adjust thread tensions to the rolled edge setting.

56

2. Lay the prestrung pearls in the channel at the front of the foot and through the tunnel in the back of the foot. Lower the foot and take two or three stitches over the strand of beads.

3. Raise the foot and place the finished edge of the fabric, right side up, under the presser foot. The edge of the fabric should be slightly to the left of the string of beads. Lower the foot.

4. Stitch length is determined by the size of the bead and the desired finished effect. Refer to "Applying Prestrung Beads onto a Finished Edge."

5. Serge the beads into place. The needle should just pierce the edge of the fabric. The beads are to the right of the fabric, and the rolled edge stitch encases the beads against the edge of the fabric. (Illus. 4.)

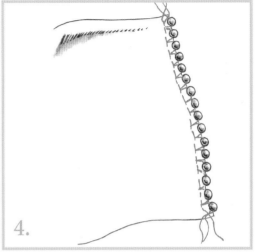

4.

6. When serging is completed, bring the thread tail ends to the back side of the project and secure.

Flatlocking Beads to Fabric

This technique is used when the beads are to lie within the body of a project. A 2- or 3-thread flatlocking stitch is serged onto a folded edge, encasing the beads within the stitch. The fabric is then unfolded, and the beads lie across the surface of the fabric.

1. Thread the serger for a 2- or 3-thread stitch. The needle position will depend on the size of the beads being serged. Adjust the thread tension for a flatlock stitch.

2. Lay the prestrung beads in the channel at the front of the foot and through the tunnel in the back of the foot. Lower the presser foot and take two or three stitches over the strand of beads.

3. Fold the fabric wrong sides together, and place it under the foot, half-way between the needle and the stitch finger. Stitch length is determined

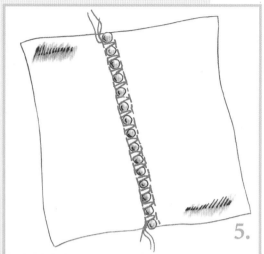

5.

by the size of the bead and the desired finished effect. Refer to step 4 "Applying Prestrung Beads onto a Finished Edge."

4. Flatlock the beads into place. When serging is completed, unfold the fabric and pull the stitch flat. Secure the thread tails by knotting or stitching them to the back of the project with a hand needle. (Illus. 5.)

Flatlocking Multiple Rows of Prestrung Beads

If the project calls for multiple rows of beads stitched close together, choose a 3 mm bead and use this technique.

1. Flatlock the first row of beads into place using the "Flatlocking Beads to Fabric" technique.

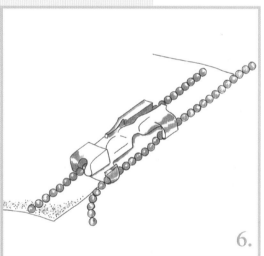

6.

2. For the second row of beads, fold the fabric, wrong sides together, ¼" or 5 mm from the first row of beads.

3. Place the previously stitched row of beads in the cording groove on the left side of the foot. The fold for the second row of beads should be positioned halfway between the right needle and the stitch finger. (Illus. 6.)

4. Lay the second string of beads in the channel at the front of the foot and through the tunnel in the back of the foot. Flatlock in place.

5. Continue to flatlock additional rows of beads in place.

Creating Beaded Serger Trim

Individual beads and semiprecious stones can be strung onto 10-lb. test monofilament line and stitched into the serger's thread chain to create a trim suitable for sewing machine couching, jewelry, or a warp "yarn" for pin-weaving.

58

1. Thread individual beads onto a medium-weight (10-lb. test) monofilament line. Do not cut the monofilament line from the spool, as the beads will be moved along this line during serging.

2. Thread the serger for a 3-thread stitch using the right needle. Raise the knife out of the way and select the rolled hem setting.

3. Adjust the thread tensions by chaining off a tail of approximately 3". Holding the thread tail firmly in the left hand keep a constant, light, pulling pressure on the tail. Tighten upper and lower looper tensions, and loosen the needle tension until the thread is fed off all three spools evenly.

4. Remove the presser foot. Lay the monofilament line on top of the thread chain, to the right of the needle. Serge a few stitches, securing the monofilament line into the thread chain. Because there is no presser foot on the machine, pull the thread tail gently while stitching, keeping constant, even tension.

5. With the needle in the thread chain and the monofilament line to the left of the needle, slide a bead to the left of the needle. Take two or three stitches without catching the monofilament line in the thread chain. Place the monofilament line to the right of the needle, and stitch it into the thread chain for approximately 1". (Illus. 7.)

6. Hold the thread chain in the left hand, the monofilament line in the right hand, and gently pull on the monofilament line, sliding the bead into place along the thread chain.

7. Continue to secure the monofilament line and the beads to the thread chain in the same manner. (Illus. 8.)

7.

8.

59

Note: Winding the serger trim onto a 6"x12" piece of heavy cardboard as it is serged will help keep the trim from tangling. (Illus. 9.)

Sequins

When selecting sequins for serger application, choose flat prestrung sequins. Cupped sequins will not move through the foot easily. Insert the sequins with the "nap" of the strand toward the stitcher. Sequins are available in a variety of sizes. Most feet will accommodate 2 mm–5 mm sequins.

9.

Securing Sequins onto a Finished Edge

This technique is used when placing sequins on the finished edge of a project.

1. Thread the serger and adjust the tensions for a balanced 2- or 3-thread stitch. The needle position will depend on the width of the strand of sequins.

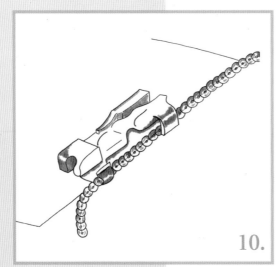

2. Raise the knife out of the way. Lay the prestrung sequins in the channel at the front of the foot and through the tunnel in the back of the foot. Insert the sequins with the "nap" of the strand toward the stitcher. (Illus. 10.)

3. Lower the presser foot and take two or three stitches over the strand of sequins.

4. Place the finished edge of the fabric, right side up, under the foot. Set the stitch length at 4, and serge the sequins into place.

10.

5. When serging is completed, hold the project in one hand and the end of the strand in the other and gently pull the serged strand. The

sequins will shift position on the fabric, sliding over the overlock stitch, hiding the threads under the sequins.

6. Secure the thread tail ends to the back.

Flatlocking Sequins to Fabric

If sequins are to be placed within the body of a project, choose a 2- or 3-thread flatlock stitch. All stitching is done on the fold of the fabric, encasing the sequins within the flatlock stitch.

1. Thread the serger and adjust the tensions for a 2- or 3-thread flat-lock stitch. The needle position will depend on the width of the strand of sequins.

2. Raise the knife out of the way. Lay the prestrung sequins in the channel at the front of the foot and through the tunnel in the back of the foot. Insert the sequins with the "nap" of the strand toward the stitcher. Lower the presser foot and take two or three stitches over the strand of sequins.

3. Fold the fabric wrong sides together, and place it under the presser foot. The fold in the fabric should be placed halfway between the needle and the stitch finger. Set the stitch length at 4, and flatlock the sequins into place. (Illus. 11.)

11.

4. When serging is completed, remove the project from under the presser foot, and clip the thread chain before the first sequin. Holding the project in one hand and the end of the strand in the other, gently pull the strand of sequins toward the stitcher. The sequins will shift position on the fabric, sliding over the flatlock stitch, hiding the threads under the sequins.

5. Gently pull the fabric so the sequins lie flat across the surface of the fabric. Bring the thread tails to the back side of the project and secure.

61

CHAPTER 7

Fashionable Accessories

From Austrian crystals to glittery sequins, the beaded accents on these simple accessories can add sparkle to any outfit for any special occasion. Just follow the instructions to add a little extra beaded elegance in any wardrobe.

MATERIALS:

- ⅛ yd velveteen
- ¼ yd medium weight fusible interfacing
- 1¼ yds of Austrian crystals molded-on-a-string (for a 33" belt)
- ½ yd black tulle or netting
- skirt type hook-and-eye closure
- embroidery floss, topstitch-ing thread, or any other strong thread
- monofilament thread
- piping foot

TECHNIQUES:

Basic couching directions, page 49

MEASURING:

Cut a strip of interfacing and a strip of velveteen on the crosswise grain 3¼" x waist measurement + 3". Fuse interfacing to the wrong side of the strip of velveteen.

Cut a 3½"x4½" piece of velveteen for the loop of the bow.

Black Tie Belt

*E*nhance a basic black dress for that special occasion. This belt is a surprising combination of velveteen and tulle mixed with glamorous Austrian crystals.

64

Instructions:

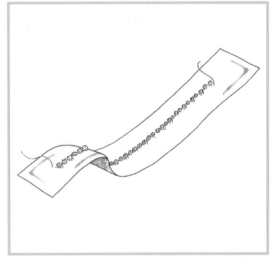

1. Using the universal stitch and a piping foot, couch the crystals down the center of the strip, starting and ending 3½" from each end. Adjust the stitch width to clear the crystals.

2. Fold the strip right sides together, and stitch, leaving a 4" opening near the center of the seam.

3. Refold the strip with the seam at the center back. Stitch across each open end of the belt. Carefully press seam open.

4. Trim the corners and turn the belt right side out. Press and close the opening by hand-stitching.

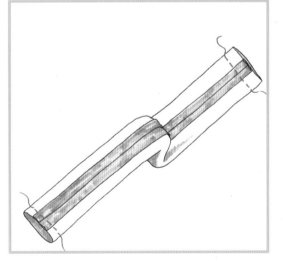

5. To make the bow, cut the tulle to 52"x18". Fold in half lengthwise. Fold in thirds lengthwise and again in thirds across the width to form a rectangle approximately 4"x8". Gather the tulle in the center and using embroidery floss, topstitching thread, or other strong thread in a hand needle, wrap the center of the bow, and knot securely.

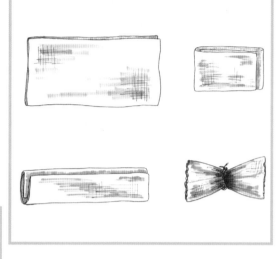

6. Fold the loop piece, right sides together, matching the $4\frac{1}{2}$" edges, and stitch down one side. Turn and press seam open.

7. Couch two rows of crystals onto the loop, $\frac{3}{8}$" in from the side edges. Start and stop $\frac{1}{2}$" from the raw edges.

8. Fold wrong sides together and stitch the raw edges together to form the loop. Finger-press the seam open, and turn the loop to the right side.

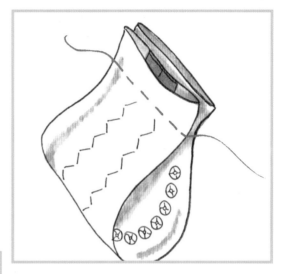

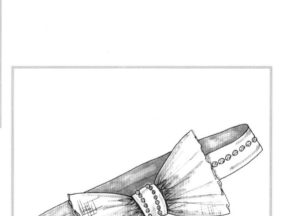

9. Bartack the loop to the belt at one end. Pull the tulle bow through the loop. Adjust as desired.

10. Sew the hook to the belt behind the loop. Sew the eye to the other end of the belt in the appropriate position.

MATERIALS:

- ¾ yd black organdy or organza
- 3 mm black molded beads
- liquid or spray stabilizer
- 3 yds of 2¼" black satin ribbon
- piping foot
- edgestitch foot
- black polyester thread
- chalk or fabric marker
- decorative cord for draw-string

TECHNIQUES:

Basic couching directions, page 49
Applying prestrung beads onto a finished edge, page 56

MEASURING:

Cut two 18" squares of the organdy. Spray or paint each square with liquid stabilizer. Let dry. Using chalk or fabric marker, draw a 16½" circle on one square of organza.

Organdy Wrist Bag

*T*his little black bag is great for evening but made in white, it becomes a bride's purse. Pastel colors and a smaller size make it a perfect accessory for a child's Easter dress.

Instructions:

1. Select a zigzag stitch, W-3.5 mm and L-3 mm. Using the piping foot, set the needle position at far left. Place the end of the string of beads under the foot, and begin stitching inside the circle. Start near an edge and meander around in a random pattern similar to the drawing, until the circle is covered with a curving strand of beads, ending near an edge.

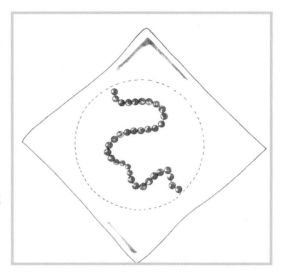

2. Place the two squares of organdy wrong sides together. Using a straight stitch, stitch along the drawn $16\frac{1}{2}$" circle, sewing through both layers. Trim around the circle, leaving a $\frac{1}{4}$" seam allowance.

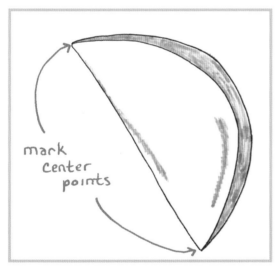

mark
center
points

3. Fold the circle in half, and mark the edges at the halfway point.

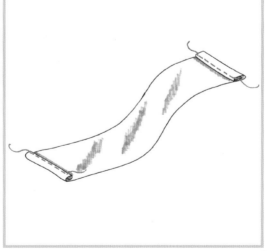

4. Cut the ribbon into four 25" pieces. On the short ends of each piece, turn under twice and stitch to hem.

5. Place two pieces of ribbon, wrong sides together, and edgestitch along one long edge. Repeat with the other two pieces of ribbon.

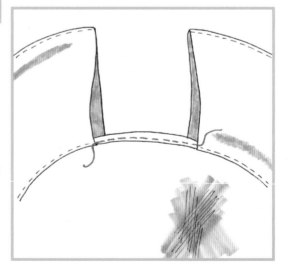

6. Starting ¼" away from one of the center marks, place stitched ribbon on the edge and pin in place, sandwiching the organdy between the ribbon. Stitch to the edge of half of the circle, using a ¼" seam allowance. Repeat with the second piece of ribbon and the other half of the circle.

7. At the two open areas where the raw edge is still exposed, clip the seam allowance to the stitching line and ¼" past the beginning of the ribbon on each side. Trim one seam allowance to ⅛" and fold the remaining seam allowance to the inside twice and stitch.

70

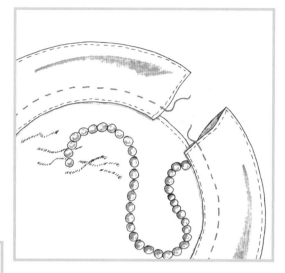

8. To form the casing for the drawstring, straight stitch through both layers of the ribbon 1½" from top edge.

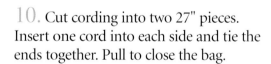

9. Using a piping foot and a zigzag stitch, couch molded or prestrung beads along the top edge of the purse.

10. Cut cording into two 27" pieces. Insert one cord into each side and tie the ends together. Pull to close the bag.

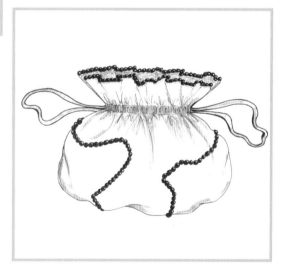

MATERIALS:

- ⅓–½ yd velvet or velveteen fabric
- ½ yd lining fabric
- 12" zipper in a color matching the fabric
- 1¼–1½ yds embroidered ribbon or trim
- 1½ yds gold sequins
- 10–12 faceted 12 mm beads
- 1 yd of gold chain with 2 jump rings
- 2 gold tassels
- zipper foot
- edgestitch foot
- open embroidery foot
- gimp cord

TECHNIQUES:

Basic couching directions, page 49
Attaching single beads larger than 6 mm, page 36

MEASURING:

Using the pattern piece, cut one from fabric and one from lining. Cut two circles of fabric, each 3". Cut the embroidered trim into five 7½" pieces. Turn each short end under ¼" and stitch. Cut two pieces of fabric each 1"x2" for the strap holders.

72

Sequined Shoulder Bag

This sequined shoulder bag is perfect for carrying the essentials for a night on the town. The zippered opening extends the full length of the purse and provides easy access to the articles inside.

Instructions:

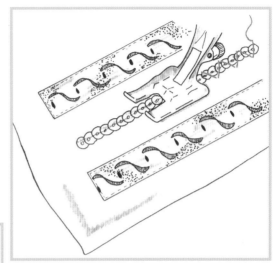

1. Position trim as indicated on the pattern, and using an edgestitch foot, stitch in place along all four sides of each piece.

2. Using an open embroidery foot, couch a row of sequins between each of the rows of the trim as indicated on the pattern.

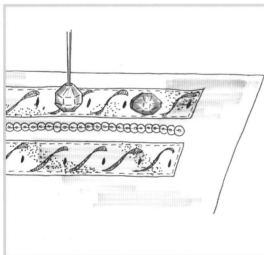

3. Using free-motion techniques, stitch the larger beads along the end pieces of trims as indicated on the pattern.

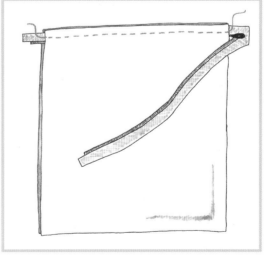

4. Place one side of the zipper face down on the right side of the short edge of the fabric. Place the lining right side down on top of the zipper with raw edges even. Using a zipper foot, stitch next to the zipper coils. Repeat on the opposite edge of the purse. Turn right side out.

5. Fold each strap holder piece right sides together along the 1" side. Stitch down the side, using a ¼" seam allowance, forming a tube. Turn to the right side and press.

6. Slip each tube through a jump ring, and fold in half to form a loop. Pin or baste in position at each end of the zipper as indicated on pattern.

7. Serge finish each end of the purse, stitching across the zipper tape and attaching the loop in the process.

8. Zigzag over gimp cord along the serged edge.

9. Fold the purse with lining side out and the zipper across the center. Partially unzip the opening. Pull the gimp cord up to gather each end and tie together.

74

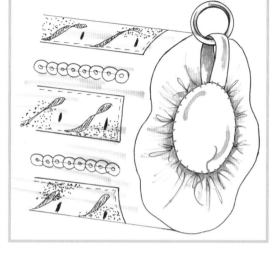

10. Zigzag over gimp cord along the outside edge of the small fabric circles, leaving about 2" of cord at each end. Pull up the gimp cord, and fold the raw edges to the wrong side of the circle. Position the circle over the gathered end of the purse. Whipstitch in place. Repeat with the other end of the purse.

Note: This process can be repeated with a circle of lining fabric on the inside of the purse if desired.

11. Attach a tassel to each end in the center of the circles.

12. Attach the ends of the chain handle to the jump rings.

75

MATERIALS:

- 20"x10" piece velvet or velveteen
- 20"x10" lining
- polyester thread to match the fabric
- 20" of 2 mm molded, cross-locked, or prestrung gold beads
- 40" of 3 mm molded, cross-locked, or prestrung gold beads
- 40" of 2 mm molded, cross-locked, or prestrung beads the same color as fabric
- 32" of decorative cord for drawstring
- ¼ yd tear-away stabilizer
- monofilament thread
- all-purpose presser foot
- zipper foot
- edgestitch foot
- piping foot

TECHNIQUES:

Basic couching directions, page 49

MEASURING:

Cut two pattern pieces from fabric and two from lining fabric. Mark the darts and the bead placement line across each fabric piece. Cut the stabilizer into ten strips, 1½"x10".

Beaded Palm Purse

Small enough to carry in the palm of the hand, this soft drawstring bag is simply decorated with couched rows of beads and finished with a hanging tassel.

76

Instructions:

1. Position a strip of stabilizer behind the marked line on one piece of fabric. Select piping foot and thread machine with nylon thread in the needle and the bobbin. Set for a zigzag stitch, W-3 mm and L-3 mm. Beginning and ending at the side seam lines, couch the 2 mm gold beads along the bead placement line. Carefully remove as much of the stabilizer as possible from the wrong side of the stitched area.

Note: Using the stabilizer in strips and removing as much as possible after each line of stitching will keep the beaded area from becoming too stiff. Some stabilizer will remain and will help the bag to form its shape. However, one large piece of stabilizer adds too much stiffness and detracts from the beauty of the bag.

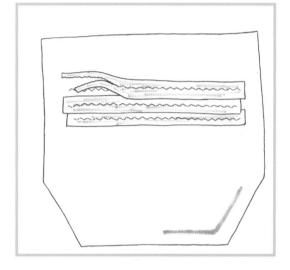

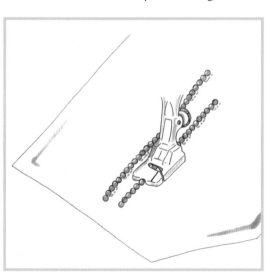

2. Couch a line of colored beads on each side of the gold beads, guiding the edge of the foot along the first line of couched beads. Carefully remove as much of the stabilizer as possible from the stitched area.

3. Couch the larger gold beads on each side of the colored beads, guiding the edge of the foot along the previously couched beads. Carefully remove as much of the stabilizer as possible from the stitched area.

77

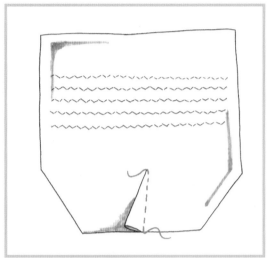

4. Using matching polyester thread and an all-purpose foot, stitch the dart at the lower edge of each fabric piece.

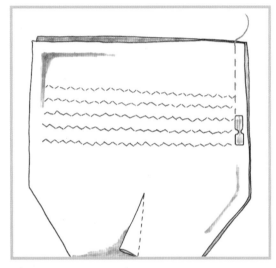

5. With right sides together, stitch one side seam on fabric pieces, using a zipper foot and left needle position. Open the seam and finger-press. Repeat for lining.

6. With right sides together, stitch fabric and lining across top edge. Press seam with seam allowances toward the lining.

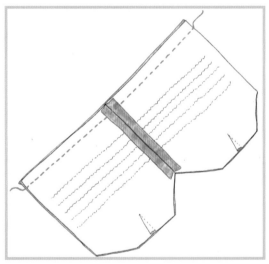

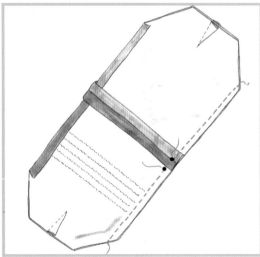

7. Fold purse lengthwise with right sides together. Stitch lining and fabric side seam, leaving the fabric open between the dots. Press seam allowance open. Do not sew the bottom seams at this time.

78

8. Fold lining down into the purse matching lower raw edges. The velvet fabric will extend over the top and down into the inside of the purse. Straight stitch on casing stitching line to form drawstring casing.

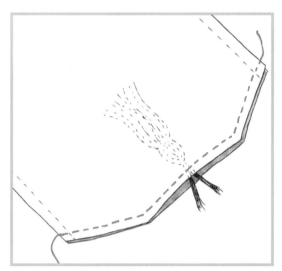

9. Pin tassel in place between layers of fabric at center of lower edge. Stitch across the bottom of the purse, securing the tassel at the same time.

10. Turn right side out through the lower opening in the lining. To close the lining opening, turn the seam allowances in, and edge stitch.

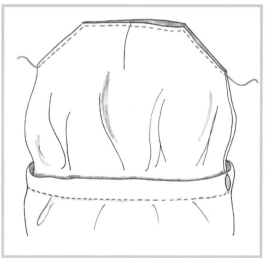

11. Thread decorative cord into the casing and pull up to close.

MATERIALS:

- ¾ yd black tulle or netting
- water-soluble stabilizer
- black lingerie thread
- white or light-colored fabric paint marker
- strands of black beads
- individual black sequins
- 2 tassels
- 2 black beading bobbins
- temporary spray adhesive

TECHNIQUES:

Attaching Single Beads 6 mm or Smaller, page 34
Attaching Charms, Single Sequins, and Treasures, page 37
Attaching a String of Loose Beads in a Straight Line, page 38
Attaching a String of Loose Beads in a Curve, page 39

MEASURING:

Trace the pattern onto water-soluble stabilizer. Pre-string beads for bangles and lower edge onto beading bobbin in correct order. Prestring beads for body onto separate bobbin.

Beaded Shoulder Toss

*T*his beaded accessory can turn an office look into evening glamour. When worn over the shoulder of a black jacket, the netting blends into the fabric, instantly adding sparkle and panache for a special look.

80

Instructions:

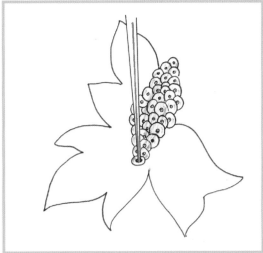

1. Spray the unmarked side of the stabilizer with the temporary adhesive. Place the stabilizer on top of the netting and smooth out all wrinkles.

2. Following pattern design, stitch sequins to netting through stabilizer.

3. Stitch a single row of beads around each group of sequins.

4. Stitch the indicated beads to the netting.

5. Couch strung beads and bangles along the neck edge and the lower edge.

6. Add tassels to the front ends.

7. Remove stabilizer by rinsing the netting with water. Dry flat.

CHAPTER 8

Exquisite Crafts

Combine beading with other craft techniques to adorn your home, make elegant gifts, or decorate for the holidays.

MATERIALS:

- ¾ yd taffeta, satin, or similar fabric
- white or off-white rayon thread
- ¾ yd lightweight fleece
- marking pen or chalk
- assortment of white and off-white individual pearls
- assortment of white and off-white pearl buttons
- ¼ to ½ yd of 3½" white or off-white double-edged lace
- ½ yd of pre-strung beads to match the fabric
- 1½" white or off-white sheer wire-edged ribbon
- 7 to 10 ribbon roses
- 1 yd of ¼" wide ribbon

Bell Pull Sampler

*U*se this elegant wall decoration to add an elegant touch to any room. Adorned with several types of beads, this bell pull is actually a sampler of beading techniques.

84

Instructions:

1. Using a fabric marker or chalk, trace the pattern markings for decorative stitching and lace onto the front fabric piece.

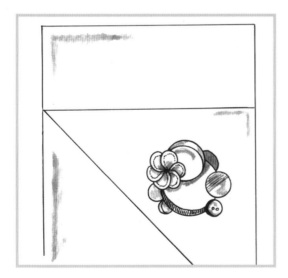

Section #1

2. Arrange buttons in a pleasing cluster and sew in place.

TECHNIQUES:

Attaching Single Beads 6 mm or Smaller, page 34
Attaching Single Beads 6 mm or Larger, page 36
Attaching a String of Loose Beads in a Straight Line, page 38
Attaching a String of Loose Beads in a Curve, page 39
Basic Couching Directions, page 49
Curves, page 50
Beading Finished Edges, page 51

MEASURING:

Cut two pieces of taffeta of the pattern piece. Set aside one for the backing.

85

Section #2

3. Position the double-edged lace as indicated and stitch each edge in place using a narrow zigzag stitch. Couch the string of colored beads across the lace in a curve loosely following the design of the lace. Add a few individual pearls and ribbon roses across the lace to complete the design.

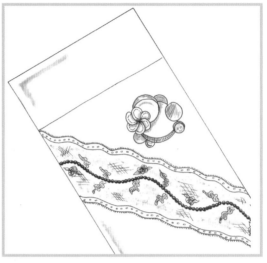

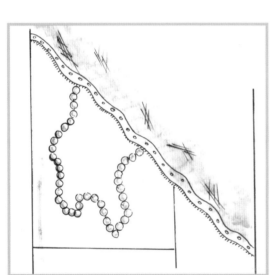

Section #3

4. Using a piping foot, couch a strand of beads in a curving, meandering design.

Section #4

5. Tie three bows using ¼" ribbon and bartack into place as indicated on the pattern. Attach a pearl in the center of each bow.

86

Section #5

6. Position three vertical rows of ¼"
ribbon as indicated on the pattern. Secure
in place temporaily using a fabric glue
stick. With a piping foot, couch strands of
pearls on top of the ribbon. If desired,
place a row of decorative stitching between
the couched rows. Stitch a ribbon rosette at
the end of each couched row.

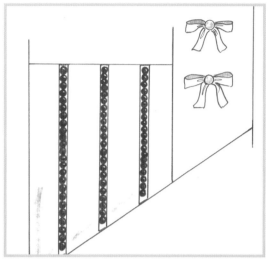

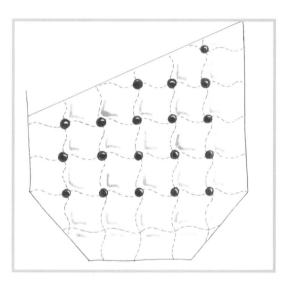

Section #6

7. Using a decorative stitch and rayon
thread, stitch a grid in the lower section as
indicated on the pattern. Stitch individual
pearls at each intersection of the grid.

8. Stitch along the marking lines dividing
the sections using a variety of decorative
stitches.

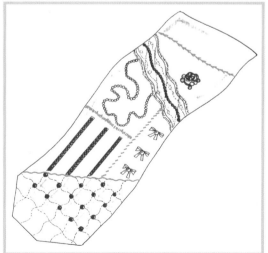

9. Place the back and the front of the bell pull right sides together. Stitch all edges, leaving the top open. Trim the seam allowances and corners and turn to the right side.

10. Baste the top edge together. Clean finish the edge with the serger or fold under ¼" and stitch close to edge.

11. Fold finished edge to the back 1½" and stitch, using a blindhem stitch on the sewing machine.

12. Slip the hardware through the casing at the top edge.

88

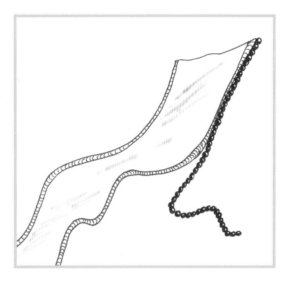

13. Using the piping foot, couch pre-strung pearls to the edge of the wire-edged ribbon.

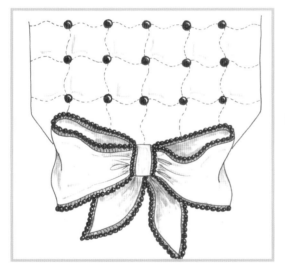

14. Tie the ribbon into a bow and stitch to the center lower edge of the bell pull.

89

MATERIALS:

- 1 yd moire taffeta
- small lace motifs
- assorted bridal pearl beads and oat pearl beads
- 1 yd flat lace edging
- ⅔ yd ribbon if using flat lace
- lingerie thread to match lace
- polyester thread to match bag fabric

TECHNIQUES:

Attaching Single Beads 6 mm or Smaller, page 34
Attaching a String of Loose Beads in a Curve, page 39

MEASURING:

Using the pattern, cut two bag sections from the moire taffeta. Lay aside one of the cut pieces to be used as the bag lining.

Lingerie Bag

*T*uck a little intimate apparel into this beaded lingerie bag for a truly unique bridal gift or as a special gift to yourself.

90

Instructions:

1. Arrange and pin the lace motifs on the bag front as desired and stitch in place using a free-motion zigzag stitch.

2. Attach the beads to the lace motifs where desired. Bead the edging lace and lay aside.

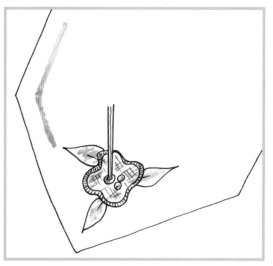

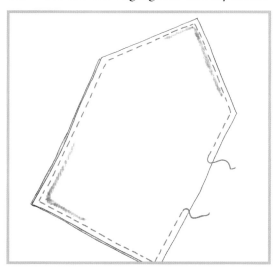

3. Stitch the bag and lining right sides together, leaving an opening on one side. Trim, turn and press.

4. Edgestitch all sides of the bag, closing the opening while stitching. Attach a small section of beaded motif at the center front.

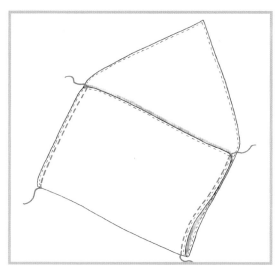

5. Gather and stitch the beaded edging to the ribbon. Stitch to the front flap edge.

6. Fold up the edge of the bag to form the pocket. Stitch along the sides to secure.

91

MATERIALS:

- 1¼ yds of 54" wide fabric or 1⅓ yd. of 45" wide fabric
- 3⅝ yds pregathered 1½" wide lace
- 4 yds molded-on-a-string beads
- 24" nylon coil zipper
- serger thread to match fabric
- decorative thread for flatlocking
- multi-purpose foot
- buttonhole foot
- gimp cord
- polyester thread to match lace
- 20" pillow form

TECHNIQUES:

Flatlocking Beads to Fabric, page 57
Flatlocking Multiple Rows of Prestrung Beads, page 58

MEASURING:

Cut a 20" square of fabric for the pillow front. For the pillow back, cut two pieces, 20"x10" each; for the ruffle, cut three strips of 54" fabric or four strips of 45" fabric, 6" wide.

Boudoir Pillow

*A*dd a feminine touch to a bedroom by creating a delicate beaded pillow for the bed. Make several, changing fabric, lace, and/or beads.

92

Instructions:

1. Following the illustration, measure, fold, and lightly crease the pillow front, to mark the placement for strands of beads.

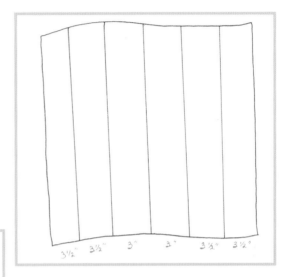

2. Baste the lace in place on the pillow front. The header of the lace should lay at the fold lines, the body of the lace should lay toward the outer edges of the pillow front.

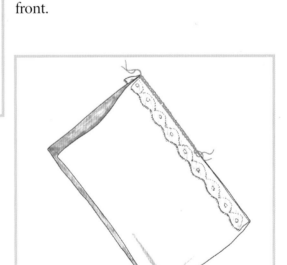

3. Adjust the serger for a 2- or 3-thread flatlock with decorative thread in the upper or lower looper, respectively. With wrong sides together, fold the pillow front along an outer crease line with the lace on top. Flatlock along the crease, encasing the header of the lace.

93

4. Continue flatlocking each piece of lace. For the center fold, a piece of lace will be against the feed dogs as well as on top of the fabric.

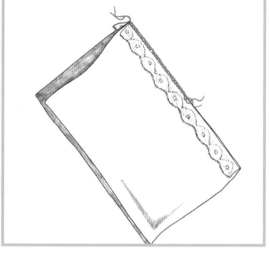

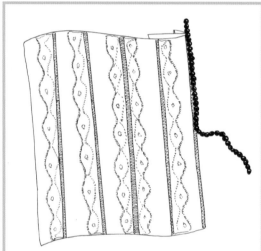

5. Rethread the serger with thread to match the fabric. With the decorative flat-locked stitch on top and the lace against the feed dogs, flatlock the beads into place. Do not cut off the excess pearls at this time. For the center rows of beading, flat-lock the first row of beading into place. Then the second row of beads is flatlocked in place.

6. Using the sewing machine, seam the ruffle strips into a cylinder. Fold in half, wrong sides together and press.

7. Gather the unfinished edge of the ruffle, by zigzaging over gimp cord.

8. Divide the ruffle and the pillow front into quarters. Pull the gimp cord to gather the ruffle. Pin the gathered ruffle sections to the pillow front matching marks adding extra gathering at the corners.

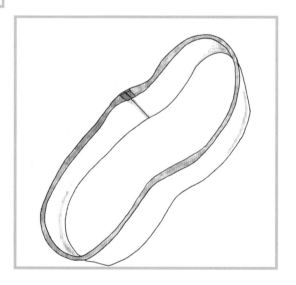

94

9. Using ½" seam allowances, stitch the ruffle to the pillow front. Hand walk the machine over the beads in the seams or remove the presser foot, lower the feed dogs and free motion stitch the seam allowances over the beads.

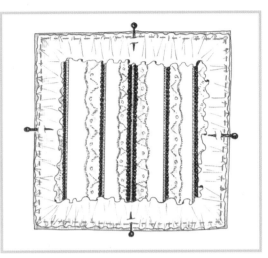

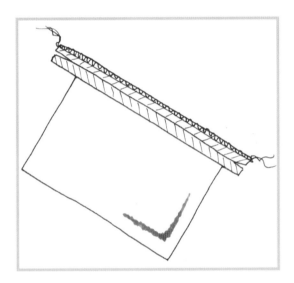

10. Adjust the serger for a balanced 4-thread stitch. Place the zipper on top of one pillow back piece, right sides together, extending at least 2" beyond the edge of the fabric. Guide the fabric and zipper under the foot so the left needle stitches about ⅛" from the zipper coil. Some of the tape and seam allowance may be trimmed. Serge in place. With the zipper on top, position the remaining back fabric under the other side of the zipper, right sides together. Serge the remaining zipper tape to the pillow back as before.

11. With the zipper partially unzipped, pin the pillow back to the front. Using a ⅝" seam allowance, stitch the back to the front. Sew carefully over the beads.

12. When all stitching is completed, trim the beads to within one bead of the seam allowance. Turn the pillow right side out and insert a 20" pillow form.

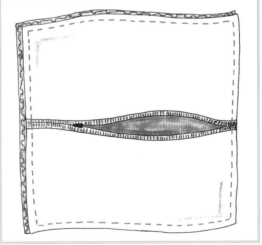

MATERIALS:

- ½ yd ivory tapestry fabric
- ¼ yd ivory moire taffeta
- ¼ yd lightweight fleece
- 2.0 mm double needle
- 1½ yds of prestrung 2 mm gold beads
- 2 spools of gold metallic thread
- lightweight bobbin thread
- 3 mm to 5 mm gold beads individual gold sequins
- large gold tassel
- piping foot
- open embroidery foot
- edgestitch foot
- fabric marker

TECHNIQUES:

Applying Prestrung Beads onto a Finished Edge, page 56
Attaching Single Beads 6 mm or Smaller, page 34
Attaching Charms, Single Sequins and Treasures, page 37

MEASURING:

Cut two stockings from the tapestry fabric. Cut two cuffs from the taffeta and cut one cuff from the fleece. With a fabric marker, transfer the stitching lines to the right side of one of the cuff pieces. Cut a 2"x7" strip of fabric for the hanger.

96

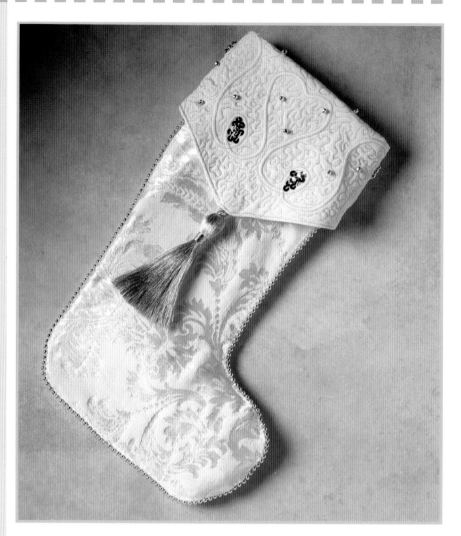

Gold and Ivory Christmas Stocking

$\mathcal{M}$ake the holiday extra special with this unlined, quilted and beaded stocking made of ivory tapestry and taffeta with gold beads and sequins.

Instructions:

1. Place the two stocking pieces, right sides together. Stitch or serge along the sides and around the foot. Turn the stocking right side out and press.

2. Using monofilament thread, piping foot and a zigzag stitch, couch the beads along the edge of the stocking, starting and ending near the unfinished top of each side as indicated on the pattern.

3. Place the fleece cuff on the wrong side of the cuff piece marked with the stitching pattern. Pin or baste in place.

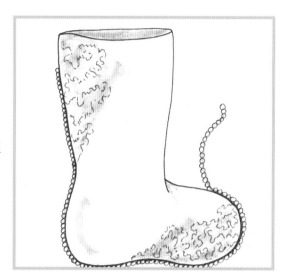

4. Thread the sewing machine with the two spools of gold metallic thread and the 2.0 mm double needle. Following the drawn pattern lines, stitch the design across the cuff.

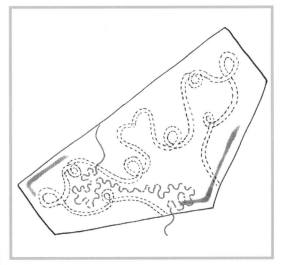

5. Rethread the machine with a single needle and one spool of gold metallic thread. Lower the feeddogs and stipple quilt the area in and around the double needle pattern.

6. Attach individual beads and sequins on the cuff.

7. Fold the embellished cuff right sides together and stitch the back seam, using a ¼" seam allowance. Repeat with the cuff lining piece.

8. Pin or baste the tassel to the cuff at the place indicated on the pattern. The tassel should be laying toward the top of the cuff.

98

9. Place the cuff and the cuff lining right sides together and stitch along the lower edge using a $\frac{1}{4}$" seam allowance. Turn right side out and press lightly. Baste the top edges of the cuff together.

10. To make the hanger for the stocking, fold the edge of the hanger strip in towards the center and fold at the center. Stitch along the open side. Pin or baste in place as indicated on the pattern.

11. Place the cuff inside the stocking (the right side of the cuff to the wrong side of the stocking) with the raw edges even. Stitch or serge along the upper edge using a $\frac{1}{4}$" seam allowance. Turn the cuff to the outside of the stocking.

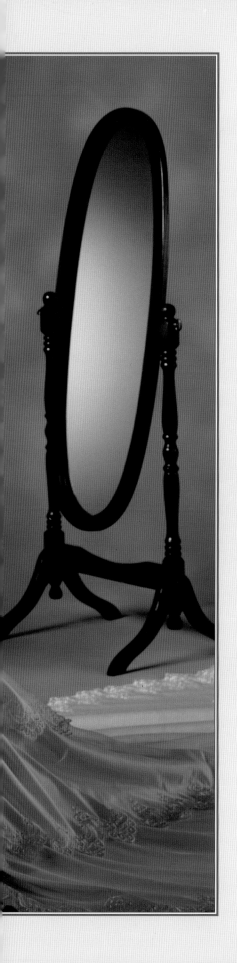

CHAPTER 9

Elegant Attire

From everyday to evening wear, beading is fashionable for any look or mood. Serge stripes of beads onto a vest, subtly embellish a soft sweater dress, or lavishly decorate a beautiful wedding gown. Add that special touch to ready-to-wear clothing or incorporate it into hand crafted garments.

MATERIALS:

- vest pattern of choice
- heavy cardboard or foam core board large enough for vest front
- long straight pins
- variety of coordinated fabrics for weaving
- variety of yarns for weaving
- lining fabric

To create 35 yds serger trim:

- 3 spools of lightweight rayon and/or metallic decorative thread
- variety of drilled precious stones, plastic and metal findings, beads, and charms
- 10-lb. test fishing line
- monofilament thread or a decorative sewing machine thread to accent the fabric choices
- darning foot or walking foot
- iron-on interfacing for the vest fronts
- Teflon® press cloth

TECHNIQUES:

Creating Beaded Serger Trim, page 58

MEASURING:

Cut or tear 1½" strips from the variety of fabrics chosen for weaving the vest front.

102

Pin-Woven Vest

*A*dd precious stones, beads, and findings to your next pin-woven garment by creating serger beading to use as a warp yarn. Small treasures peeking from between the woven strips and serged decorative thread adds an extra element of elegance and interest to the project.

Instructions:

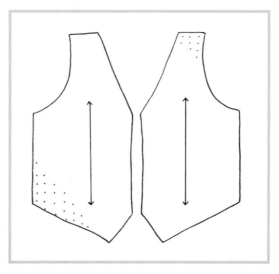

1. Following pattern instructions, cut the vest back and lining pieces. Cut two vest fronts from iron-on interfacing. Mark grain lines on the adhesive side of each interfacing piece. Label the pieces "right front" and "left front" accordingly.

2. Fold each 1½" wide strip of fabric lengthwise into thirds and press so that no raw edges show.

103

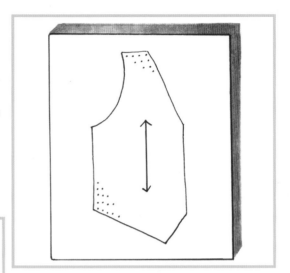

3. Pin one of the interfacing vest fronts on the cardboard or foam core, adhesive side up. Center to allow for equal pinning space around the pattern piece.

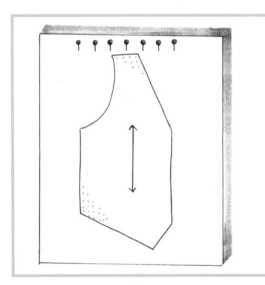

4. Beginning 1" above the shoulder line, place a pin in the cardboard. Angle the pin away from the body. Place angled pins at ½" intervals across the upper edges of the interfacing, 1" beyond the edges of the piece.

5. To position the first pin along the lower edge of the interfacing, draw a straight line from the pin to the lower edge of the vest. This line should be parallel to the grain line on the interfacing piece. Place an angled pin at the end of this line and at ½" intervals, 1" below the lower edge of the interfacing.

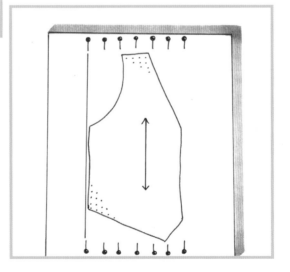

104

6. When all pins are in place, begin stringing the serger trim between the pins. Anchor the end of the trim as illustrated off the edge of the interfacing. Wrap the trim around each pin, keeping the trim taunt between pins. Reposition pins if necessary. When all wrapping is complete, cut the trim and anchor the end off the edge of the interfacing.

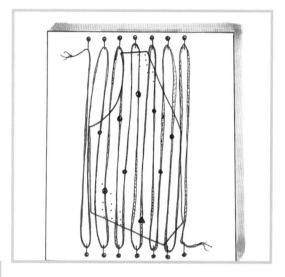

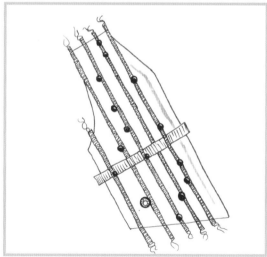

7. Beginning in the middle of the interfacing piece, weave the fabric strips between the serger trim in an over and under fashion. Weave the second strip of fabric in an alternating manner.

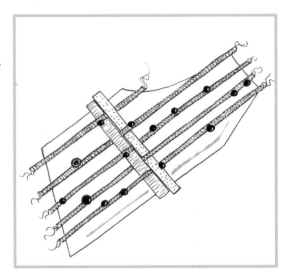

8. As additional fabric strips and yarns are woven into the serger trim, snug them close to the previously woven row. Mix fabric colors and yarns in the weaving process to create interest and varied textured patterns. As the weaving progresses, turn the stones, beads, and findings on the serger trim to lie to the top.

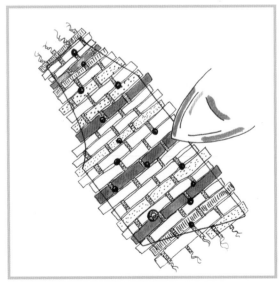

9. To hold the weaving in place before stitching, carefully press (not iron) the woven strips to the interfacing, using a dry iron and a Teflon® press cloth. Do not press any bead or finding that may melt or discolor. Carefully press the outer edges of the interfacing.

10. Secure the weaving to the interfacing by stitching through the woven strips. Choose monofilament thread if the stitching is not being used as a decorative accent on the garment. Choose a rayon or metallic decorative thread if additional color will enhance the design of the weaving. Use a walking foot and any running stitch on the machine, or lower the feed dogs and secure the strips by free motion stippling using a darning foot. Avoid stitching too closely to any of the stones and findings on the serger trim.

11. Position the original pattern piece on the interfaced side of the weaving and pin in place. Trim away the excess weaving. Check to see that the edges are firmly secured to the interfacing. Press and stitch again if necessary.

12. Following steps 3 through 10, weave the other interfacing vest front.

13. Following the vest pattern instruction sheet, complete the construction of the lined vest. Handle each vest front piece carefully when stitching.

MATERIALS:

- purchased sweater knit dress, *or*
- pattern suitable for sweater knits and sweatering fabric and ribbing as required by pattern
- water-soluble stabilizer
- temporary spray adhesive
- fine point permanent ink marking pen or fabric paint marker
- lingerie-type thread to match the color of the bridal pearls
- 3 mm bridal pearls
- size B beading bobbin
- 5 mm bridal pearls for flower centers
- light table

TECHNIQUES:

Attaching Single Beads 6 mm or Smaller, page 34

Attaching a String of Loose Beads in a Straight Line, page 38

Attaching a String of Loose Beads in a Curve, page 39

MEASURING:

Cut out sweater pattern sections following pattern directions. Handle the sweatering as little as possible to avoid stretching.

108

Sweater Dress

*E*mbellish a simple sweater dress and create an elegant evening garment by adding beading. Use these techniques when creating your own garments or as an enhancement to purchased sweatering.

Instructions:

1. If the beading design is to cross seam lines, stitch the necessary seams before continuing. If the beading does not cross seam lines, working with individual pattern pieces will be easier.

2. Cut two pieces of water-soluble stabilizer larger than the beading design pattern. Using a dry iron and a dry press cloth, press the layers together to form one layer.

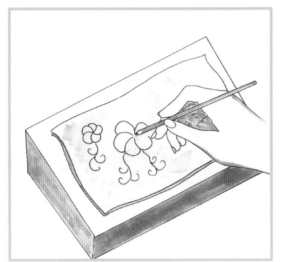

3. Using a marking pen and a light table, trace the design onto the stabilizer. Apply spray adhesive to the unmarked side of the stabilizer.

109

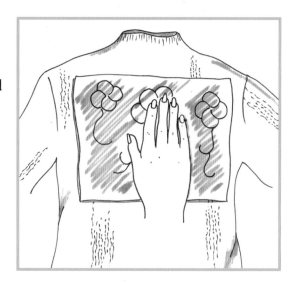

4. Place the adhesive side of the stabilizer against the right side of the sweatering and carefully smooth the stabilizer into place. Avoid stretching the sweatering by hand pressing, not rubbing, the stabilizer to the fabric.

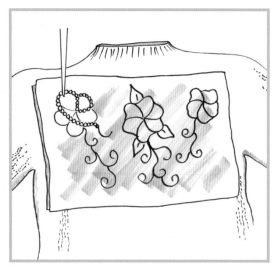

5. Stitch the beads to the sweatering, following the technique directions. Follow the drawn design for accurate bead placement. Bead the flower centers last.

110

6. When all beading is completed, remove as much of the water soluble stabilizer as possible by cutting it close to the stitching with appliqué or sharp embroidery scissors. Do not tear the stabilizer away from the sweatering, doing so may break the stitches and stretch the sweatering. Do not remove the remaining stabilizer until construction is completed.

7. Following pattern instructions, construct the garment.

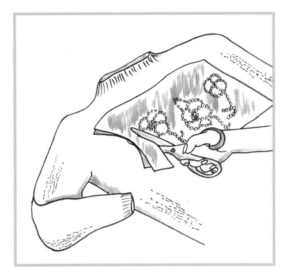

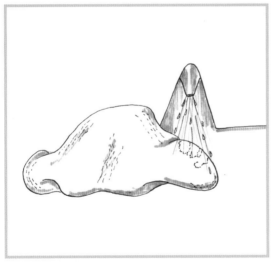

8. Remove any remaining stabilizer by turning the garment inside out and rinsing under cool running water.

9. Lay the garment flat to dry. Lightly steam if necessary.

MATERIALS:

- fabrics, linings, interfacings, and notions as required by the pattern
- nylon lace motifs
- lace edging for the lower edge of the gown
- assortment of bridal pearls and oat pearls
- assortment of iridescent individual sequins
- bridal tulle
- monofilament thread
- lingerie thread

TECHNIQUES:

Attaching Single Beads 6 mm or Smaller, page 34
Attaching Charms, Single Sequins, and Treasures, page 37
Attaching a String of Loose Beads in a Curve, page 39
Attaching Bangles, page 39

MEASURING:

Cut out the gown and the lining, following pattern directions.

Wedding Gown

*W*hen preparing for her special day, every bride wants a one-of-a-kind gown, crafted with her in mind. Creating a custom-designed beaded dress for today's bride can also mean creating an heirloom gown to be worn by generations of future family brides.

112

Instructions:

Bodice

1. Stitch the shoulder seams of bodice and bodice lining. Stitch the bodice lining to the neck edge of the bodice of the gown. Trim and clip the neck seam. Understitch. Press the lining into place.

2. Place the bodice on a dress form. Beginning at center front neck edge, pin the motifs to the bodice fabric only, not

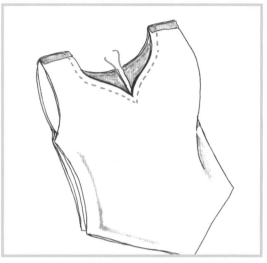

the lining fabric. Trim sections of the lace to build the design. The motif edges may extend beyond the neck edge and carry them across the shoulder line and onto the back of the dress. They should not extend below the lower edge of the bodice. When all are arranged, remove the bodice and pin the lining out of the way so it will not be caught when stitching the lace or beads.

3. Working from the center front outward and down, free motion zigzag the lace motifs to the bodice. Do not stitch into the zipper area or down onto the armhole edge.

4. Attach beads and sequins to the bodice as desired. Do not attach beads or sequins to the zipper area or the armhole edge.

The Sleeves

1. Cut out the upper section of the sleeve from bridal tulle. Attach the lace motif away from the sleeve seam allowance using a free motion zigzag. Bead the lace motifs.

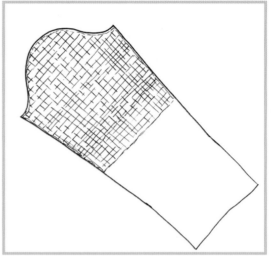

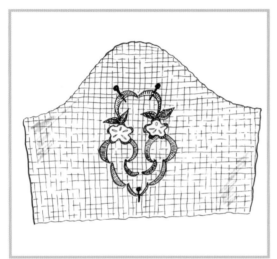

2. Lay the wrong side of the beaded bridal tulle on top of the right side of the sleeve fabric. Using a free motion zigzag, stitch around the outer edge of the lace motif.

3. Trim excess tulle from around the beaded motif. From the wrong side, carefully trim the sleeve fabric from behind the bridal tulle and beaded lace motifs.

4. Complete as much beading as possible before stitching the sleeve seams closed and stitching the sleeves into the dress. After the sleeves are stitched to the bodice, complete stitching the bead motifs and sequins to the armhole area.

The Skirt

The lace motifs on the skirt and the train were beaded before they were attached to the fabric.

1. Place the lace motif under the presser foot and stitch the individual beads and sequins to the motif.

2. Pin the beaded motifs to the skirt and train and using a free motion zigzag stitch, secure the motifs to the gown.

3. In areas where rows of beading are desired, stitch the lace motifs to the gown and then bead the motifs.

4. Stitch skirt to bodice. Add a row of couched beads at the seam line. After the skirt is sewn to the bodice and the zipper is inserted, finish stitching the lace motifs, the beads and sequins to the back of the dress. When beading around the zipper, remember the zipper must freely move up and down.

The Edging Lace

All beading was completed on the edging lace before it was sewn to the lower edge of the gown.

1. After serge finishing the lower edge of the gown, pin the lace into place and using a free motion zigzag, stitch the beaded lace edging to the gown

115

MATERIALS:

- simple cardigan jacket pattern with princess lines
- lace yardage for jacket
- interfacing
- satin underlining and lining
- lace yardage allowing for pattern matching
- tulle for sleeve underlining
- lingerie thread or monofilament thread
- 2 mm and 2.5 mm loosely strung bridal pearls
- size B beading bobbins
- small seed beads
- clear, iridescent individual sequins
- assortment of loose bridal pearls and oat beads

TECHNIQUES:

Attaching Single Beads 6 mm or Smaller, page 34
Attaching a String of Loose Beads in a Curve, page 39
Attaching Charms, Single Sequins and Treasures, page 37

MEASURING:

Cut lining, eliminating sleeve pieces. Cut sleeves from lace, matching and planning lace designs across the jacket. Cut sleeve underlining from tulle. Cut interfacing and satin underlining.

116

The Beaded Jacket

*W*hen looking for an alternative to the traditional wedding gown for a garden wedding or an elegant outfit for a silver or golden anniversary party, consider selecting a simple cardigan jacket pattern, overlaying the fabric with a layer of exquisite lace, and enhancing the lace with bridal pearls and seed beads.

Instructions:

1. Construct the jacket lining following pattern instructions. Construct a sleeveless jacket from underlining. Layer the wrong side of the lace front pieces over the right side of the underlining. Position interfacing in appropriate places. Baste pieces together.

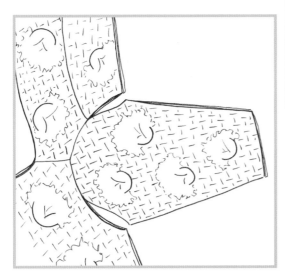

2. Mark the jacket front and neck seam allowances with a basting stitch. Mark the jacket hem in the same manner. Baste sleeve underlining to lace sleeve and mark the hem.

3. Set the sleeve into the jacket across the cap from the front notch to the back notch. Leave the remainder of the sleeve armhole open for beading. Do not stitch the underarm seam.

4. Study the lace and overall jacket design to determine which areas should be enhanced by beading.

5. With the jacket lying as flat as possible, begin beading the lace. Do not bead into the marked seam allowances or below the marked hem.

6. Once all beading is complete, continue constructing the jacket following the pattern instructions.

117

MATERIALS:

- bridal veil pattern
- bridal tulle as required by the pattern
- 3 spools of serger thread to match the veil fabric
- water-soluble stabilizer
- molded-on-a-string oats or pearls–yardage determined by the size of the veil
- hand sewing needle
- multipurpose foot for the serger

TECHNIQUES:

Applying Prestrung Beads off the Finished Edge, page 56

MEASURING:

Following pattern directions, cut the veil from the bridal tulle. Cut the water soluble stabilizer into 1" strips for veil.

Bridal Veil

Quickly add a designer touch to the bride's veil using the serger and molded oat or pearl beading. The beading will frame the bride's face and help to control the delicate bridal tulle.

118

Instructions:

1. Set the serger for a 3-thread balanced stitch; right needle; CW- 2 and L-3.

2. Place narrow strips of water-soluble stabilizer under edge of veil; serge all edges. Trim excess veil and stabilizer close to serging. Don't tear stabilizer from tulle as stitching will pull away from edge of the veil.

3. Set serger for 2- or 3-thread rolled edge and serge beads to edge. Do not bead edge of veil around head piece.

4. Trim excess beading even with unbeaded edge of veil. Do not trim stitching. The serger thread tails will be stitched under headpiece.

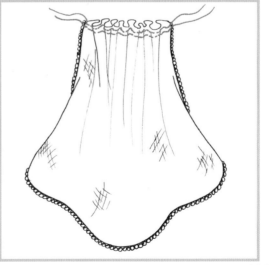

5. Stitch two rows of basting stitches along unbeaded edge of all layers of veil. Do not back stitch at beginning, but shorten stitch length and then backstitch several times at end of each basting row.

6. Gather edge of veil by pulling on the unsecured threads.

7. Gather veil to fit headpiece and hand stitch, catching serger thread tails into whip stitching.

CHAPTER 10

Lasting Treasures

*W*ith proper care and attention, most beaded garments and items can become heirlooms to be handed down from generation to generation.

Care and Storage

Cleaning, pressing, and storage of beaded items requires knowledge of the fabric and beads to ensure the proper treatment.

Because of the delicate nature of the beads and attached embellishments, items such as wedding dresses, christening gowns, and first communion dresses need more specialized care than most garments and craft projects. All projects will eventually need cleaning, so it is wise to check fabric, thread, and beads for care compatibility. Fabrics that need to be dry-cleaned should be embellished with threads and beads that will withstand dry cleaning chemicals. Fabrics that are machine or hand washable and/or dryer safe should be decorated with threads and beads that are also washable and/or dryer safe.

To test, cut two 6" square swatches of the proposed fabric and, using the chosen thread, stitch at least one of each type and color of the selected bead and/or charm onto each swatch. Launder or dry-clean one swatch, keeping the other one for comparison. Have the dry cleaner process the swatch three or four times. If the project is to be washed, wash the swatch several times. If the garment will be dried in the dryer, dry the swatch after each washing. Compare the original swatch with the one that has been through the cleaning process. Have the beads discolored or faded? Are the metal findings as bright as the original? Do the threads still hold the beads firmly in place? If the answer to any of these questions is no, choose a different fabric, change the thread choice, and/or experiment with different beads and charms.

To protect the beaded item, launder machine-washable garments on a gentle cycle within a lingerie bag. Take care to turn all washable garments inside out before cleaning. Protecting the beading while cleaning the garment will mean fewer broken or loose beads to be repaired. Even if the fabric is machine dryable, it is recommend that beaded garments be hung to dry.

If pressing is necessary, always work from the wrong side, using a press cloth. Lay a thick towel on the ironing board before pressing any beaded article. The beads settle into the towel and are protected from the iron.

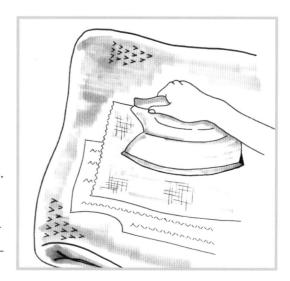

Care should always be used in cleaning garments because many beads are very delicate and breakable. Ask the dry cleaner to take extra care when handling beaded projects.

Most dry cleaners offer a special service for wedding dresses that includes cleaning, wrapping, and boxing the garment for storage. This process is recommended for any beaded project that is to be stored away for a long time.

To prepare an item for storage, check to see that all beads and charms are securely attached and that the item is freshly cleaned and pressed. Wrap the item in acid-free tissue paper to protect it from chemicals in the air, light damage, and discoloration. Blue tissue paper will also help to keep a white item from turning yellow. Storing an item in plastic is not a good idea because it doesn't allow the fabric to breathe. Lack of air will eventually destroy the fibers.

There may be some items such as a wedding hat or christening gown that will make a pretty display. Place the freshly cleaned and pressed item under a glass dome or in a glass case to protect from dust and airborne particles. Take care to display it away from strong light to avoid yellowing and fading.

Even though the process of machine beading takes a fraction of the time of hand beading, the planning and stitching of a lovely beaded garment or project automatically gives it the status of an heirloom. Using the proper care and storage techniques will add years to the life of these projects and create enjoyment for generations to come.

123

Glossary

Abalone—shell used for beads; often used to inlay designs into plain beads. Also known as paua shell in New Zealand

Agate—Made up of fibrous quartz, opal, and chalcedony; beads are often made from this semiprecious stone

Amber—fossilized gum from trees millions of years old; its color ranges from yellow to deep red

Amethyst—Greek for "not drunken"; this purple quartz was thought to prevent drunkenness

Annular—ring-shaped bead

Bakelite—an early plastic invented in 1909; it was used to imitate other materials, such as jet, amber, and ivory

Barrel—cylinder-shaped bead with tapered or rounded ends

Bead—object shaped from hard material with a hole going through it for stringing or attaching

Bicone—beads that form a triangular shape at each end

Bugle Beads—small tubes; these beads can be opaque, transparent, pearlized (called Ceylon) or satin-finished for a matte finish

Cabochon—dome-shaped stones with flat backs

Cane—a rod of colored glass shaped and melted together with others to form decorative glass beads known as Venetian glass

Carnelian—this form of chalcedony was thought by the Egyptians to be a symbol of life because of its blood-red color

Ceramic Bead—made of clay and baked until hard, these beads can be decorated and finished for a variety of looks

Charm—made of metal or metal-looking plastic, these shaped pieces have a ring or hole for attaching

Chalcedony—decorative quartz

Cinnabar—of Chinese origin; carved, black wooden beads stained with a red color to resemble the mineral cinnabar

Cloisonné—metal beads with designs outlined with thin metal strips and filled in with enamel paint

Cone—bead that is usually flattened on one end and triangular shaped on the other

Copal—cheaper than amber, this is a semifossilized resin

Coral—the skeleton of sea creatures, this material comes in various shades of red

Cylindrical—shaped as a cylinder, this long, rounded bead is one of the most popular shapes

Diamanté—a glass bead made with numerous facets to create glitter and sparkle;. also known as rhinestone in the United States

Disk—flat circle of material with hole through it

Drop—tear shaped, the hole in this bead is drilled through the length or at the top

Facet—a flattened surface made by cutting or molding the bead—these catch the light and reflect it to create sparkle

Faience—an early ceramic material developed by the ancient Egyptians

Filigree Bead—ornamental work

Garnet—one of the hardest gemstones, dark red in color

Inlay—designs of one material embedded into another

124

Jet—black beads made from this mineral similar to lignite; popular in Britain in the 19th century

Lampwork Bead—bead made by wrapping molten glass around a wire and heating it over a lamp

Lapis Lazuli—semiprecious stone made up of grains of several blue minerals

Lustering—a glazing process developed in 9th century Baghdad, it gives ceramic beads a metallic luster

Malachite—a green gemstone often imitated in glass

Millefiori—meaning "thousand flowers," these Venetian beads are fused from layers of colored glass and resemble a flower when cut in a cross-section

Monofilament Thread—nylon invisible thread that is a lightweight version of fishing line

Mosaic Beads—built up of sections of different colors of glass, making these the most ornate of beads

Mother-of-Pearl—the iridescent lining of a shell, often carved into beads

Oats—beads shaped like a grain of oat

Oblate—a bead that measures larger around the diameter than the length

Opaque—nontransparent, unable to be seen through

Pearls—created by oysters when an irritant, such as a grain of sand, lodges inside it and is covered by a calcium carbonate substance. Cultured pearls are made by purposely placing the irritant inside the shell. Imitation pearls are made of glass or plastic and painted with a pearlized finish

Pipe—a bugle or tubular bead

Polymer Clay—a plastic clay that is baked after being shaped into beads; can be painted after baking to add color and pattern.

Porcelain—hard white translucent clay fired at high temperatures

Powder Glass Beads—African beads made from pulverized recycled glass; they have a soft granular feel to them

Quartz—silica, the most common rock material. Many semiprecious stones are forms of quartz

Rhinestone—American term for diamanté

Rhodonite—a reddish gemstone, named for the Greek rose, "rhoden"

Rocaille Beads—French for "little stone," these beads are round and made of glass. Sometimes called pound beads because they were once sold by the pound.

Rock Crystal—colorless quartz

Rose Quartz—cloudy pink in color

Round Bead—spherical-shaped bead

Segmented Bead—bead that has several parts, such as a collar around the holes of the beads

Semiprecious—gemstones such as jade, lapis, and agate used for beads.

Sequins—flat metal, metal-looking plastic, leather, or vinyl, these discs have a hole through the center for attaching. Also come in strand form. Can be cupped with facets.

Tabular Beads—flat beads with a hole drilled through the center

Transparent—not opaque, it can be seen through

Tubular—bead shaped like a tube with the hole going through the length

Turquoise—aqua-colored stone meaning "Turkish stone"

Venetian Glass Beads—originally made in Venice, these ornately colored beads are made of several colors of glass canes molded and melted together

Vulcanite—made in the early 1900s of a sulphur-treated rubber

125

Pattern Section

Inches	MM	CM	Inches	CM	Inches	CM
⅛	3	0.3	9	22.9	30	76.2
¼	6	0.6	10	25.4	31	78.7
⅜	10	1.0	11	27.9	32	81.3
½	13	1.3	12	30.5	33	83.8
⅝	16	1.6	13	33.0	34	86.4
¾	19	1.9	14	35.6	35	88.9
⅞	22	2.2	15	38.1	36	91.4
1	25	2.5	16	40.6	37	94.0
1¼	32	3.2	17	43.2	38	96.5
1½	38	3.8	18	45.7	39	99.1
1¾	44	4.4	19	48.3	40	101.6
2	51	5.1	20	50.8	41	104.1
2½	64	6.4	21	53.3	42	106.7
3	76	7.6	22	55.9	43	109.2
3½	89	8.9	23	58.4	44	111.8
4	102	10.2	24	61.0	45	114.3
4½	114	11.4	25	63.5	46	116.8
5	127	12.7	26	66.0	47	119.4
6	152	15.2	27	68.6	48	121.9
7	178	17.8	28	71.1	49	124.5
8	203	20.3	29	73.7	50	127.0

Metric Equivalents — Inches to Millimetres and Centimetres (MM – millimetres, CM – centimetres)

Metric Conversion Chart

Yards	Inches	Metres	Yards	Inches	Metres
⅛	4.5	0.11	1⅛	40.5	1.03
¼	9	0.23	1¼	45	1.14
⅜	13.5	0.34	1⅜	49.5	1.26
½	18	0.46	1½	54	1.37
⅝	22.5	0.57	1⅝	58.5	1.49
¾	27	0.69	1¾	63	1.60
⅞	31.5	0.80	1⅞	67.5	1.71
1	36	0.91	2	72	1.83

126

Chapter 7
Palm Purse
1 square = 1 inch

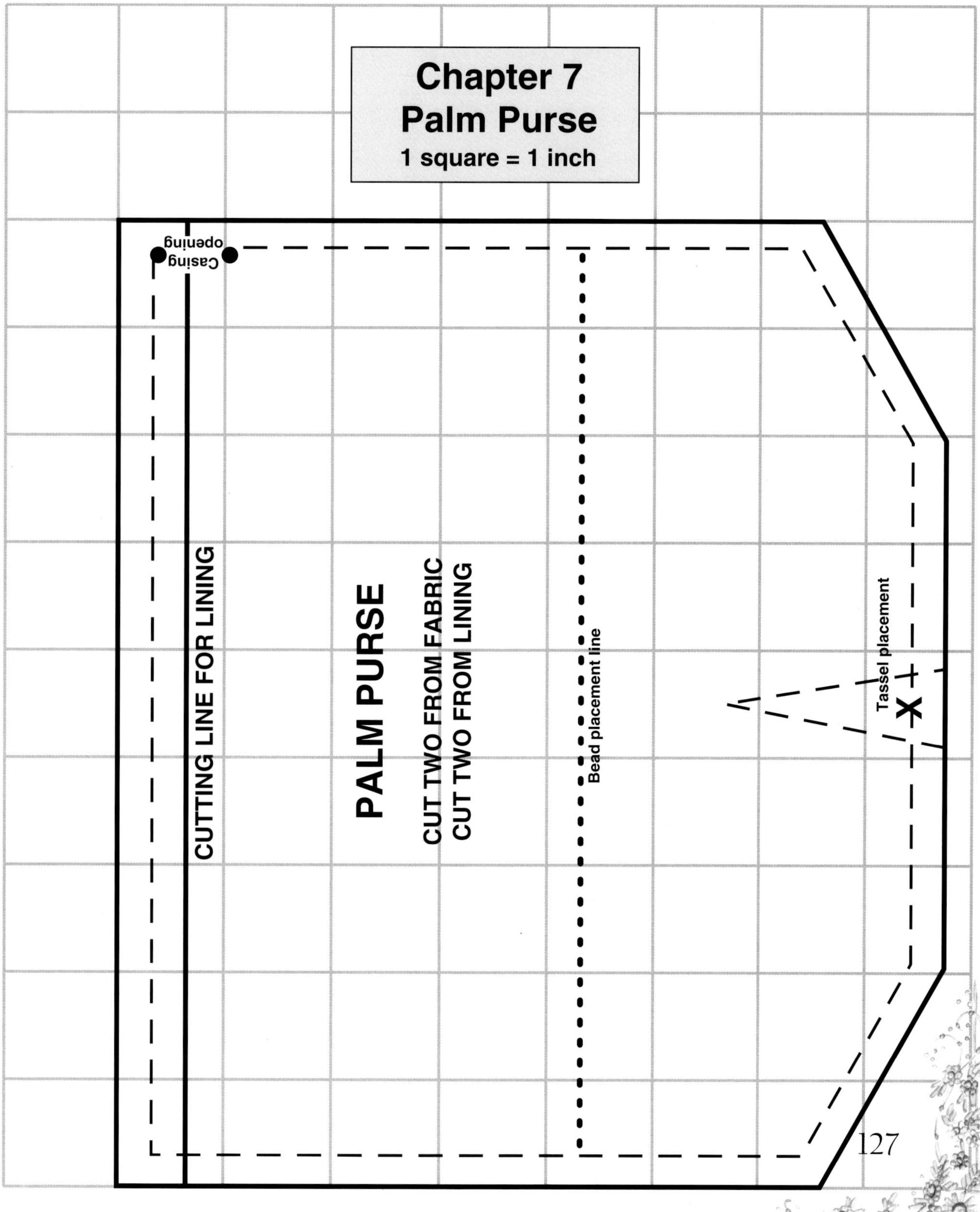

Casing opening

CUTTING LINE FOR LINING

PALM PURSE

CUT TWO FROM FABRIC
CUT TWO FROM LINING

Bead placement line

Tassel placement

X

127

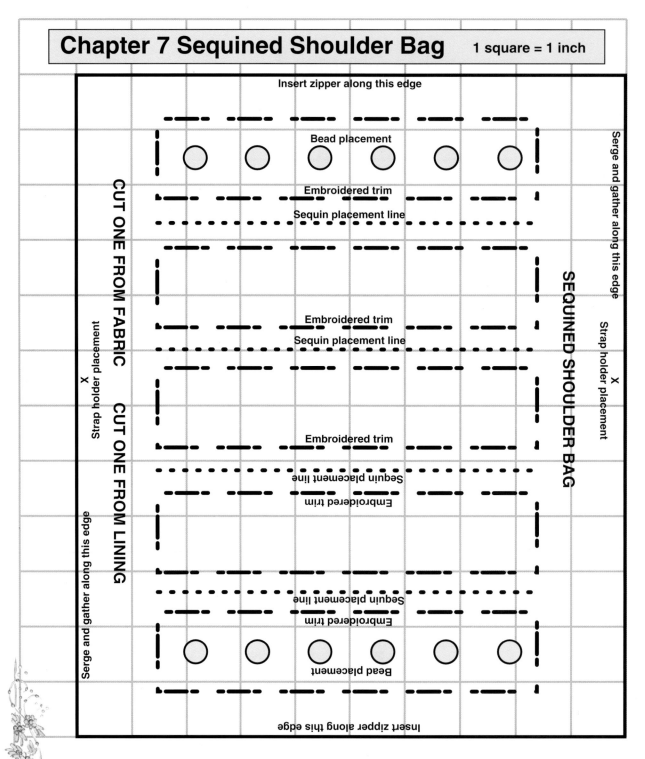

Chapter 7 Sequined Shoulder Bag 1 square = 1 inch

Insert zipper along this edge

Bead placement

Embroidered trim

Sequin placement line

Embroidered trim

Sequin placement line

Embroidered trim

Sequin placement line

Embroidered trim

Sequin placement line

Embroidered trim

Bead placement

Insert zipper along this edge

CUT ONE FROM FABRIC   CUT ONE FROM LINING

X
Strap holder placement

Serge and gather along this edge

Serge and gather along this edge

X
Strap holder placement

SEQUINED SHOULDER BAG

128

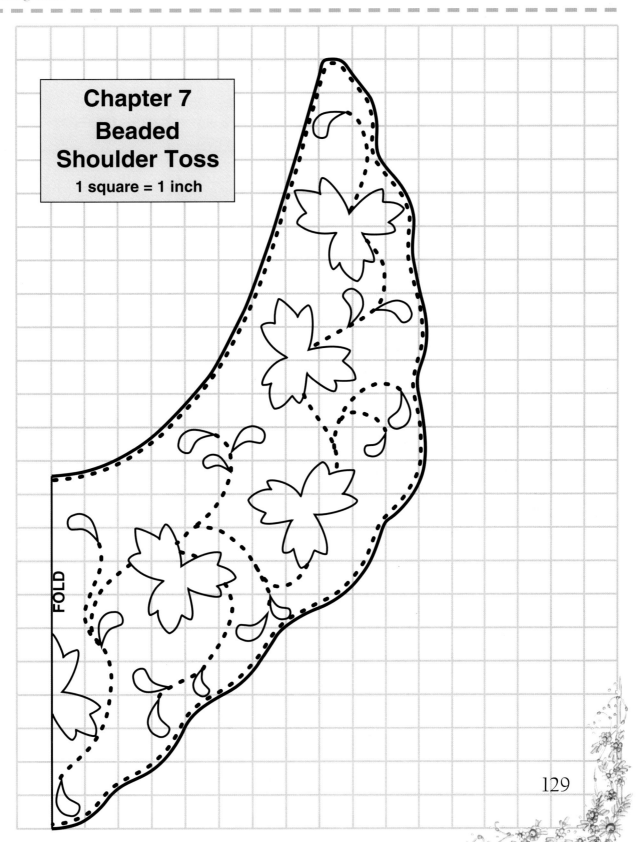

**Chapter 7
Beaded
Shoulder Toss**
1 square = 1 inch

FOLD

129

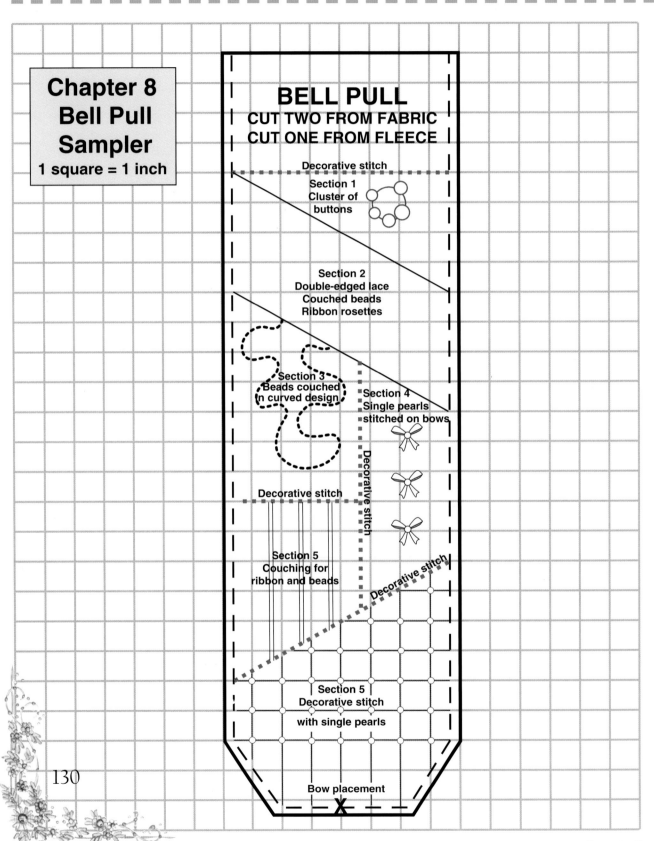

**Chapter 8
Bell Pull
Sampler**

1 square = 1 inch

BELL PULL
CUT TWO FROM FABRIC
CUT ONE FROM FLEECE

Decorative stitch

Section 1
Cluster of
buttons

Section 2
Double-edged lace
Couched beads
Ribbon rosettes

Section 3
Beads couched
in curved design

Section 4
Single pearls
stitched on bows

Decorative stitch

Decorative stitch

Section 5
Couching for
ribbon and beads

Decorative stitch

Section 5
Decorative stitch

with single pearls

Bow placement

130

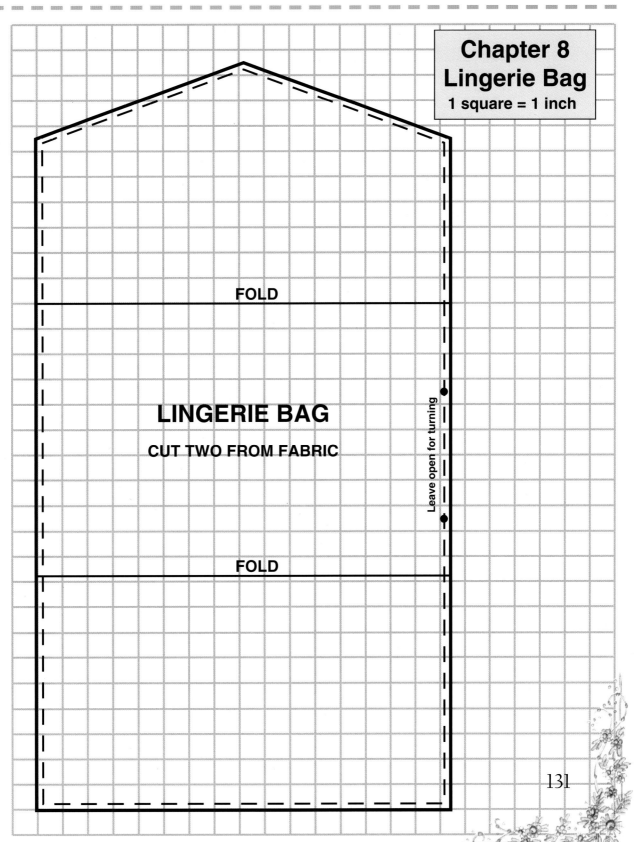

**Chapter 8
Lingerie Bag**
1 square = 1 inch

FOLD

LINGERIE BAG

CUT TWO FROM FABRIC

Leave open for turning

FOLD

131

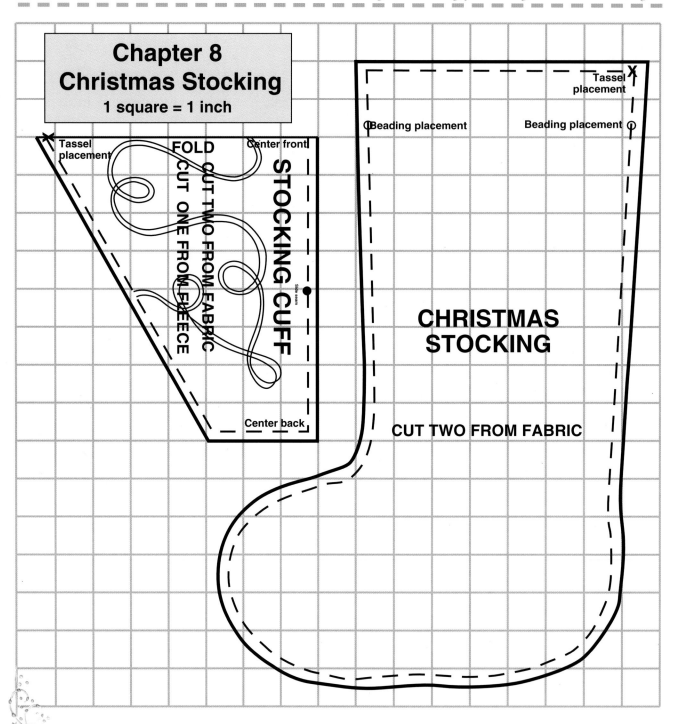

**Chapter 8
Christmas Stocking**
1 square = 1 inch

Tassel placement

FOLD

Center front

CUT TWO FROM FABRIC
CUT ONE FROM FLEECE

STOCKING CUFF

Side seam

Center back

Tassel placement

Beading placement

Beading placement

Tassel placement

**CHRISTMAS
STOCKING**

CUT TWO FROM FABRIC

132

Index

135